CASEMATE |

THE SOVIET BATTLE FOR BERLIN, 1945

IAN BAXTER

CIS0045

Published in 2025 by
CASEMATE PUBLISHERS
1950 Lawrence Road, Havertown, PA 19083, USA
and
47 Church Street, Barnsley, S70 2AS, UK

Print Edition: ISBN 978-1-63624-437-2
Digital Edition: ISBN 978-1-63624-438-9

Design by Battlefield Design
Maps on pages 26, 33, 61 and 62 by Battlefield Design
Printed and bound in the Czech Republic by FINIDR s.r.o.

CASEMATE PUBLISHERS (US)
Telephone (610) 853-9131
Fax (610) 853-9146
Email: casemate@casematepublishers.com
www.casematepublishers.com

CASEMATE PUBLISHERS (UK)
Telephone (0)1226 734350
Email: casemate@casemateuk.com
www.casemateuk.com

All photos contained in this book are derived from archival sources, including the U.S. National Archives and Records Administration, Library of Congress, Bundesarchiv, and the U.S. Military History Institute, unless otherwise noted.

Author's note: Geographic names are given as they were during World War II and do not reflect current usage.

Author acknowledgements: I wish to thank my artist Oliver Missing for his time and expertise in producing some fine and well-detailed German and Soviet tanks. Please find Oliver's vast selection of illustrations at his "Engines of WW2" site: www.o5m6.de. I also wish to thank my Brazilian soldier artist, Renato Dalmaso, who is an illustrator and comic book artist. He works mainly with watercolor and gouache on paper and illustrates the war comic projects *The Elísio: A Journey to Hell and Jambocks*, as well as four comic book albums telling the stories of the Flamengo and São Paulo football clubs. He also works as an illustrator and cover artist for several publications in Europe and Brazil: renatodalmaso@gmail.com.

Title page image: An elderly Volkssturm POW, captured on the Seelow Heights.
Contents page image: A column of T-34s advances to Berlin.
Contents page map: Soviet artillery formations from a contemporary map.

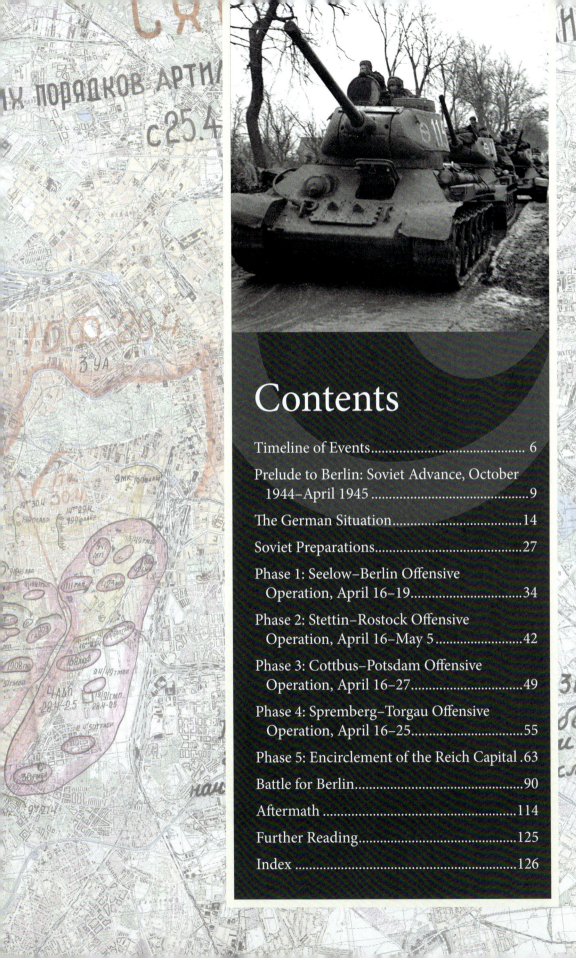

Contents

Timeline of Events

The Berlin strategic offensive operation was far greater than the battle inside the capital itself. The preparation for the battle for the German capital began as early as January 1945 and saw three massive Soviet fronts advance through the Baltic States, East Prussia, Poland, and into Germany. The Red Army then secured bridgeheads along the Oder River, broke defenses at "Fortress Kurstin," the gateway to Berlin, and secured positions in front of the Seelow Heights. From these well-defended German lines the Soviets went on to complete the encirclement of the city before the final battle that ensued inside Berlin.

January 12, 1945: 1st Belorussian and 1st Ukrainian Fronts launch the Red Army's winter offensive, the Vistula–Oder offensive.

January 14, 1945: 2nd Belorussian Front attacks through East Prussia and advances into Pomerania.

January 24, 1945: 1st and 2nd Belorussian Fronts begin the East Pomeranian offensive.

January 25, 1945: 1st Belorussian Front cuts off the fortress city of Poznan defended by 65,000 German troops; Red Army advances west to the Oder, covering up to 60 miles a day.

January 28, 1945: The two-month siege of fortress city Küstrin begins. The city, the gateway to Berlin, is situated on the Oder just east of the Seelow Heights.

March 6, 1945: Hellmuth Reymann is appointed commander of the Berlin Defense Area. Preparations for the defense of Berlin begin.

March 20, 1945: Himmler is replaced by Gotthard Heinrici as commander of Army Group Vistula.

April 2, 1945: Stavka orders 1st Ukrainian Front to advance in the Cottbus area south of Berlin and annihilate enemy positions there, then to advance to the River Elbe.

Volkssturm march through the streets of Berlin bound for the front lines.

A Soviet T-34 tank advances along a Berlin street.

April 6, 1945: Stavka directs 2nd Belorussian Front to strike northwest of Berlin and drive 3rd Panzer Division against the Baltic coast.

April 6, 1945: Stalin gives 1st Belorussian Front's Zhukov full responsibility of coordinating the strategic offensive against Berlin. Hitler orders Busse's 9th Army to stand firm in the defense of the Seelow Heights.

April 10, 1945: 1st Belorussian Front begins establishing positions along the Oder from Frankfurt in the south to the Baltic, into the Seelow Heights. 2nd Belorussian Front deploys north of the Seelow Heights.

April 15, 1945: Hitler transfers command of the Berlin city defense from himself to Army Group Vistula.

April 16, 1945: The Seelow–Berlin offensive operation opens with a million troops of the 1st Belorussian Front attacking the Seelow Heights.

April 16, 1945: The Stettin–Rostock offensive operation opens. 2nd Belorussian Front strikes enemy defenses along the Oder, depriving the 3rd Panzer Army of movement to Berlin.

April 16, 1945: 1st Ukrainian Front opens Cottbus–Potsdam offensive operation, to destroy German positions in the Cottbus region south of Berlin. 1st Ukrainian Front also launches Spremberg–Torgau offensive operation.

April 17, 1945: Soviet 1st and 2nd Guards Tank Armies are committed to the battle of the Seelow Heights. Heavy congestion at the bridgeheads prevents full impact against German 9th Army.

April 17, 1945: German counterattack against 1st Ukrainian Front at southern perimeter near Forst is repulsed.

April 19, 1945: 1st Belorussian Front advances despite heavy losses. 4th Guards Tank Army and 5th Guards Army smash through German defensive positions, bypassing Spremberg from the south.

April 20, 1945: Spremberg is surrounded on three sides.

April 21, 1945: 1st Ukrainian Front reduces German defense on the Neisse River wrenching open a path toward Berlin.

April 21, 1945: Polish 2nd Army in bitter fighting at Bautzen.

April 22, 1945: 2nd Belorussian Front secures a 10-mile-deep bridgehead on the west bank of the Oder.

April 23, 1945: 5th Shock Army and the 1st Guards Tank Army attack German LVI Panzer Corps toward Berlin from the southeast.

April 24, 1945: Red Army offensive near Schwedt widens their bridgeheads between Gartz and Stettin.

April 24, 1945: Elements of 9th Army and 4th Panzer Army retake Bautzen.

April 25, 1945: 1st Ukrainian Front tank armies seal the fate of the enemy at Cottbus in the southwestern sector of Berlin

April 25, 1945: 6th Guards Mechanized Corps crosses the River Havel and links up with 328th Division, 47th Army, 1st Belorussian Front, completing the final encirclement of Berlin from the west and the Cottbus–Potsdam offensive operation.

April 25, 1945: 5th Guards Army troops meet American soldiers from the 69th Division, U.S. First Army south of Torgau on the Elbe River. The Spremberg–Torgau offensive operation is done.

April 26, 1945: Stettin falls to 2nd Belorussian Front who now drives west to Prenzlau, forcing 3rd Panzer Army to retreat.

April 26, 1945: 8th Guards Tank Army fights its way through the southern suburbs of Berlin to attack Tempelhof Airport.

April 27, 1945: Remnants of the German Müncheberg and Nordland divisions are pushed back to the center of Berlin with Soviets assaulting along the main axes from the southeast, along the Frankfurter Alle and south along Sonnenalle toward the Belle-Alliance-Platz and the Potsdamer Platz.

April 28, 1945: 2nd Belorussian Front has advanced some 180 miles, clearing enemy formations in northwestern Pomerania, Mecklenburg, and Brandenburg, and crippling the 3rd Panzer Army.

April 29, 1945: 3rd Shock Army crosses the Moltke Bridge in Berlin, attacking toward the government buildings including the Ministry of the Interior.

April 30, 1945: At dawn Soviets strike the Reichstag. 3rd Shock Army and 8th Guards Army attack along Wilhelmstrasse, cutting off hundreds of German troops around Tiergarten.

April 30, 1945: Hitler commits suicide in the Reich Chancellery Führerbunker.

May 1, 1945: Hans Krebs of the High Command of the Wehrmacht delivers a written letter of surrender under a white flag to Chuikov, commander of the 8th Guards Army.

May 2, 1945: Weidling meets Chuikov and signs the terms of surrender of the Berlin garrison. The battle of Berlin ends.

May 3, 1945: The 3rd Panzer Army surrenders to the British Army.

May 5–7, 1945: 12th and 9th Armies withdraw across the Elbe and surrender to the Americans.

Prelude to Berlin: Soviet Advance, October 1944– April 1945

During the summer and winter offensives of 1944, the Red Army deduced that they had destroyed or captured some 96 German divisions and 24 brigades and encircled some 219 divisions and 22 brigades. In total Heer, Waffen-SS, and Luftwaffe field divisions had lost an estimated 1,600,000 men, 6,700 tanks, 28,000 guns and mortars, and 12,000 aircraft. By December 1944 the German war machine on the Eastern Front was no longer capable of replacing its losses.

By the beginning of the last winter on the Eastern Front, the Red Army had redeployed its powerful units in the north along the borders with Finland and was making sweeping attacks in northern Norway. The Baltic States had more or less fallen, but dogged, fanatical German resistance by 34 divisions continued. A number of these German units managed to escape the pending slaughter and clawed their way into East Prussia along the Goldap–Augustow line. Farther south along the Narew and Vistula Rivers, powerful Soviet units had secured several bridgeheads and captured large swathes of territory between Rozan, Magnuszew, and Sandomierz. The Red Army objective was the Reich capital, Berlin. In front of the Soviets were the still-dangerous German Army Group Center and Army Group A. Opposing the Germans were the 1st and 2nd Belorussian and 1st Ukrainian Fronts, all quite aware that the while the enemy did not have the necessary manpower or war plan to go over to the offensive, they would nevertheless resist bitterly.

In late 1944, the Soviet High Command of the armed forces, Stavka, drew up plans, having deduced that to move against Berlin it would first need to isolate and destroy enemy formations that might pose a problem in its main objective.

A Panther tank on the edge of a decimated town during the East Prussian offensive, known as the *Gumbinnen* operation, October 1944.

In Profile:
Volkssturm Conscripts with Panzerschreck and Panzerfaust

Volkssturm conscript with Panzerschreck, Aldershof, Eastern Berlin, March 1945. (Renato Dalmaso)

A Volkssturm conscript wearing typical civilian dress. Although obscured by his weapon, he will be wearing the black Volkssturm armband on his left arm. He is armed with the Panzerschreck *Raketenpanzerbüchse* 54 (Rocket Anti-Armor Rifle Model 54, abbreviated to RPzB 54), an 8.8 cm reusable antitank rocket launcher. These weapons were used extensively in the defense of Berlin.

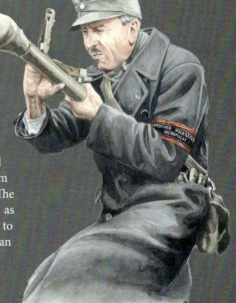

Volkssturm conscript with Panzerfaust, Müncheberg, March 1945. (Renato Dalmaso)

During training in the small town of Müncheberg, a member of the Volkssturm is armed with a Panzerfaust. The Volkssturm uniform was often very simple; it included a black armband with the lettering "Deutscher Volkssturm Wehrmacht" (German People's Storm Armed Forces). The government did attempt to issue as many of its members as possible with military uniforms, ranging from Feldgrau to camouflage types. This soldier is wearing the standard German greatcoat and M43 field gray cap.

A whitewashed PzKpfw IV withdrawing to another line of defense, late 1944.

This included pinning and reducing German forces in East Prussia. Simultaneously, the 2nd and 3rd Belorussian Fronts were tasked with attacking positions west of Warsaw, down to Poznan, and then swinging round in the direction of Berlin. The 1st Belorussian and 1st Ukrainian Fronts still fighting along the Vistula were ordered to support the other fronts for them to successfully drive back and contain the enemy along the Oder River.

In East Prussia, the Soviet offensive was decisive in paving the way for an attack on Berlin. It was here that German authorities began preparing their civilians and troops for the Soviet invasion—the *Gumbinnen* operation—as various towns along the border were attacked in what was the first East Prussian offensive in October 1944. The initial assaults were carried out by the 3rd Belorussian Front as part of the 1st Baltic Front's Memel offensive. However, the Red Army was surprised by the staunch German defense and as a result sustained massive casualties while trying to penetrate East Prussia. But over the next couple of weeks, the 1st Baltic and 3rd Belorussian Fronts eventually succeeded in pushing the German 3rd Panzer Army back to the East Prussian border, surrounding the city of Memel, and driving its forces rapidly to the shores of the Kurland ("Courland" or "Curonian") Lagoon. Although the Soviet offensive was successful, the borders of East Prussia remained solidly defended by various Heer, Waffen-SS, Allegemeine-SS, Hitlerjugend, and Volkssturm units together with local militia, postal defense units, and groups of newly raised antitank gunners. It would not be until January 13, 1945 that the 2nd and 3rd Belorussian Fronts unleashed their

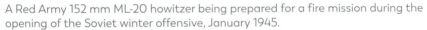

A Red Army 152 mm ML-20 howitzer being prepared for a fire mission during the opening of the Soviet winter offensive, January 1945.

A Soviet mortar crew setting up positions to attack a village, winter 1944/45.

winter offensive, the second East Prussian offensive, against the 3rd Panzer Army of Army Group North.

By January 24, after a series of heavy battles, advanced tank units of the 2nd Belorussian Front reached the Vistula Lagoon, cutting the entire 4th Army in half, along with several divisions of the 2nd Army which were trapped in what became known as the Kurland Pocket.

Soviet forces advancing on the city of Küstrin, February 1945. The city was known as the gateway to Berlin and was situated on the Oder River just east of the Seelow Heights.

Soviet riflemen supported by a T-34 tank in action in East Prussia. By end of January 1945, German forces were contained in East Prussia, allowing the main Soviet strategic offensive operation to be conducted against Berlin.

With German forces in East Prussia relatively safely bottled up, the main Soviet strategic operation was now diverted to Berlin. During February and March, the 2nd Belorussian and parts of the 1st Belorussian Front managed to destroy enemy formations defending eastern Pomerania in what was known as the East Pomeranian offensive. This successful offensive managed to remove the enemy threat of a flanking attack from the north into the rear of the armies aimed at Berlin. At the same time, unrelenting fighting raged to expand the bridgehead over the Oder west of Küstrin.

The success of the Red Army was swift. In January, the Eastern Front was still deep in Poland. Now in February, Upper Silesia was lost. German divisions in East Prussia had either retreated or were annihilated, while remnants were fighting for

A Soviet 82 mm mortar crew poses during a fire mission against German targets.

survival. In West Prussia and Pomerania, Soviet forces reported that towns and cities were being defended by a motley collection of depleted troops that had been simply thrown together. As for the defense of the Oder, it was now entrusted to Wehrmacht formations that had been fighting defensive actions for months in Poland along the Vistula.

Soviet troops on the outskirts of Küstrin, February 1945. In a desperate attempt to halt the Soviet advance toward Berlin, Hitler ordered fortress status to be conveyed on the city.

| The German Situation

By March 1945 it had become apparent to the German High Command that the main defense on the Eastern Front would be east of Berlin. The German front in the center had been wrenched wide open, allowing Soviet forces to pour through. Along two hundred miles of the defensive front, the remaining German divisions (with their handfuls of antitank and artillery guns) were strung out and almost totally unprotected.

A report noted that each division had to hold a frontage of approximately twenty miles. For every one mile of front, some units had one artillery piece, one heavy machine gun, two light machine guns, and about 150 men. For every two and a half miles of front, they had, in addition, one antitank gun. For every four miles they had one Panzer, and for every six miles one battalion. They were facing an three enemy tank armies consisting of thousands of tanks. Against this massive Soviet force was the German 9th, 4th Panzer, and 17th Armies that fielded some 400,000 troops, 4,000 artillery pieces, and 1,200 tanks. However, many of these divisions were badly depleted and conscripts drafted to the front were often 50–60-year-old men or 16–17-year-old teenagers. German commanders estimated there to be some 50–60 Soviet divisions in front of them. Army Group Vistula, comprising the 3rd Panzer and 9th Armies, was directly responsible for the immediate defense of the approaches to Berlin.

Many of its defenses had been erected on the western bank of the Oder River along a 230-mile front from Berg-Dievenow on the Baltic down to the mouth of the Neisse River. These forces comprised of nineteen infantry, four panzer, and six grenadier divisions, supported by one infantry brigade and one infantry combat group. In Army Group Center the 4th Panzer Army, 17th Army, and elements of the 1st Panzer Army were deployed along a 420-mile front from the mouth of the Neisse River to Ratibor, against powerful divisions of the 1st Ukrainian Front. The Army Group included 16 infantry, six panzer, and three panzergrenadier divisions. Also spread across the region of Breslau southeast of Berlin were numerous German battle groups supported by large numbers of Volkssturm units and subunits, with a total combined strength of some 43,000 men, 540 guns, and 120 tanks.

German troops and civilians digging antitank trenches in front of Berlin, probably February 1945.

In Profile:
General Gotthard Heinrici
December 5, 1886–December 10, 1971

Heinrici was probably one of the best generals of World War II and was considered by Hitler as a master in defense. During the war on the Eastern Front, he contributed extensively as a defensive expert and was considerably successful with various defensive strategies against the Red Army. On March 20, 1945, Hitler replaced SS-Reichsführer Heinrich Himmler with Heinrici as commander of Army Group Vistula on the Eastern Front. The situation at that time along the Oder River was precarious and it was Heinrici who was charged with seeing that the defenses there were strengthened. Yet, despite his ideological differences with Hitler and many of the General Staff, he was to try to forge one of the strongest defensive lines ever erected during the war. However, Heinrici was a realist, and he knew that the defenses he built and the forces he had at his disposal were not going to withstand the imminent Soviet onslaught. In one of the military conferences held in the Führerbunker in early April 1945, he told Hitler: "I do not believe the forces on the Oder Front will be capable of resisting the enormous attacks that the Russians are going to launch against us. The forces we have now are just shavings of the former military capacity of our army. Most of the front units have neither adequate training nor combat experience. Many of the officers are simple civil servants with no training and have been promoted in a hurry. To this we must add the lack of ammunition and all kinds of weapons and reserves." Hitler's response was simply that he was going to send large numbers of forces to the area, and that they would have plenty of time to be trained. Heinrici knew that the words from his Führer were nothing more than an illusion. Yet, despite how he felt about the war situation he was not outwardly pessimistic. Instead, dutybound, he left Berlin to plan and fortify the front with what weaponry and men he had at his disposal.

Farther south, defending positions along a 600-mile front from Banska Bystrica to Osijek was German Army Group South, comprising the 8th, 6th, and 2nd Armies. It was the task of the 2nd and 3rd Ukrainian Fronts to prevent the German forces from moving north to assist in the defense of the capital.

The main focal point of defense was the west bank of the Oder River east of Berlin. In this area all villages and towns were transformed into powerful strongholds—a dense network of trenches and a variety of resistance strongpoints where obstacles were erected to stop or slow attacking troops. German engineers also employed the sluices on the Oder River and prepared several areas for flooding.

In front of these German forces stood a huge array of military might. The 1st Belorussian and 1st Ukrainian Fronts outnumbered their enemy by a 10:1 ratio in tanks and

15

Volkssturm digging antitank ditches outside Berlin, March 1945.

self-propelled artillery, and 9:1 in artillery and troops. In the 1st Belorussian Front alone the Soviets dwarfed their enemy with infantry, tanks, and artillery; in fact, it was bigger than the entire Wehrmacht on the Eastern Front.

However, despite enemy superiority the Germans were determined to try and hold their positions for as long as possible and prevent the Soviets from taking possession of German territory east of Berlin. But despite dogged resistance in many places the Germans no longer had sufficient means to defend their positions effectively. The 3rd Panzer Army, which Hitler had relied on to hold back the main Soviet drive on the capital from the north, only had 11 depleted divisions left, while the 2nd Belorussian Front boasted 8 armies totaling 33 rifle divisions, 4 tank and mechanized corps, and 3 artillery divisions plus a powerful mix of artillery and rocket-launcher brigades and regiments. The Germans were dwarfed by enemy superiority but continued to fight from one fixed position to another.

Young members of an antiaircraft searchlight unit in Berlin. Many of these *Flakscheinwerfer* searchlights were taken out of city service in late March 1945 and moved to the Seelow Heights to be utilized against ground targets.

Volkssturm troops armed with a variety of weapons, including the Panzerfaust, marching through Berlin in a propaganda parade orchestrated by Joseph Goebbels. The Volkssturm had a total strength of 60,000 men in the Berlin area and were formed into 92 battalions, of which about 30 battalions of Volkssturm I (i.e., with weapons) were moved to the front lines, while those of Volkssturm II (without weapons) remained in the city to defend their meager positions.

With Berlin now directly threatened by a ground attack in the Seelow Heights, Hitler, now entombed 50 feet below the Reich Chancellery in his Berlin bunker, ordered flak guns—the majority of which were taken from the Berlin air defense—to be quickly emplaced east of the capital to be used in the ground role. Behind the plain on the plateau of the Seelow Heights, he had already ordered engineers to build three belts of defensive emplacements reaching back to the outskirts of Berlin. These positions nearer to the capital were called the Wotan Line, comprising a series of antitank ditches, antitank gun emplacements, and an extensive network of trenches and bunkers. Civilians from Berlin had been drafted in their thousands to assist engineers in the task of digging and constructing antitank ditches and strongpoints. To bolster the defense, Hitler had promised Heinrici 100,000 troops. However, by mid-April, only 35,000 troops had materialized, comprised mainly of untrained Luftwaffe and Kriegsmarine personnel.

General Hellmuth Reymann, appointed commander of the Berlin Defense Area in early March 1945, discusses defenses with members of the Volkssturm. Through March and early April, he undertook planning for the defenses of Berlin which included antitank ditches to the east of the city. (Bundesarchiv Bild 146-1995-081-13A)

In Profile:
German Tiger II and Panther Tanks

Panzerkampfwagen Tiger Ausf. B, 502nd Heavy Panzer Battalion, Seelow Heights, April 18, 1945. (Oliver Missing)

The schwere Panzerabteilung 502 only received a few King Tiger IIs and eight of them went into combat in early April and fought east of Berlin. This Tiger has received a sand base color and is painted in a camouflage scheme of olive-green and brown patches complete with green and brown dots. The tactical number "322" is painted in brown with a yellow outline.

PzKpfw V Ausf. G Panther medium tank, Clausewitz Panzer Division, 12th Army, April 19, 1945. (Oliver Missing)

This Panther was incorporated into an ad hoc unit of various other vehicles from a hodge-podge of panzer brigades and regiments that were simply thrown together as a *Panzersturm*. The Panther received a sand base color and is heavily painted in a camouflage scheme of olive-green and brown. Its tactical number "424" is painted in red with a thin white outline.

The German position in the East was dire. Because there were no further overriding objectives, the troops would be left along the defensive belts to prolong the war for as long as possible. Hitler expected the main attacks to be launched in the Seelow region and so all available ammunition, supplies, weapons, and armor were moved to the area in preparation. On April 15 Hitler transferred command of the city of Berlin to Army Group Vistula. Prior to this date, the defense of the capital had been directly under his command. That night (during a heated war conference) General Hellmuth Reyman, who in March 1945 had been appointed commander of the Berlin Defense Area, was told that all bridges and other facilities in the city were to be destroyed under Hitler's new scorched-earth policy. Reyman, however, contested that the policy would probably have no military value inside Berlin, and would lead to massive civilian deaths and the total economic collapse of the city. Heinrici, who was also present at the conference, agreed and also added that such a "drastic" order would prompt him to halt fighting in the city and withdraw the 9th Army toward the West.

Both Reyman and Heinrici appeared totally aware of the worsening situation in front of Berlin. Yet, astonishingly, some members of the German General Staff did not hold the same belief. They were convinced that victory could still be achieved, openly saying that nowhere else on the Eastern Front was so heavily defended and well equipped than the Berlin front. Their optimism was partly distorted by reports that five Red Army divisions with 200 tanks had tried unsuccessfully to storm the Seelow Heights west of Küstrin. However, during the last weeks of the war, German intelligence was often limited regarding the presence and disposition of the enemy forces. But what was known was a forewarning of the growing danger of a massive Soviet offensive against the Seelow Heights. German commanders in the field knew they did not have sufficient forces to defend their lines for any appreciable length of time. Consequently, plans were drawn up to withdraw and shorten the defensive positions to prevent encirclement and destruction.

Throughout April 15, along the German front soldiers were increasingly becoming aware of the looming danger. Intelligence monitored increased enemy activity. German soldiers prepared their positions with what they had at their disposal. The defenses were manned along the defensive belts comprising foxholes, trenches, and bunkers, and were supported by antitank and antiaircraft strongpoints and miles of various other obstacles. The strength of the German defenses varied. Where the main Soviet attack was predicted, soldiers were heavily concentrated along the narrowest frontage. However, these German lines of defense were in the main thinly emplaced, under-armed, and undermanned. As a result, the soldiers were dutybound to defend their position to the last man knowing that they had diminishing supplies of weapons and ammunition. The lack of armored support was another problem that manifested itself along the front and brought considerable apprehension for Heinrici, who was under no illusions as to the gargantuan nature of the task ahead. He had expressed his concerns openly with his field commanders; he worried for his men. However, worryingly for the general, the Führer's expectations were the opposite to his own. He looked upon the orders being sent from the Reich Chancellery as unrealistic and unachievable. He knew his men who were defending positions in front of the Reich capital would face calamitous consequences.

In Profile:
General Freiherr Hasso von Manteuffel
January 14, 1897–September 24, 1978

Manteuffel was a German baron from the Prussian von Manteuffel family who became a well-decorated general of the Knight's Cross of the Iron Cross with Oak Leaves, Swords and Diamonds. On both the Western and Eastern Fronts, Manteuffel was regarded as an armored warfare expert whose strategies on the battlefield had earned him the nickname "Panzer Baron." On March 2, 1945, he was ordered to report to Hitler after commanding the 5th Panzer Army on the Western Front during the Ardennes offensive. As a tactical commander in both defensive and offensive actions, he was told to assume command of the 3rd Panzer Army on the Eastern Front, one of the armies that made up the new Army Group Vistula. The Prussian aristocrat felt dutybound to undertake

preparations in slowing the Red Army's remorseless drive and to defend the banks of the Oder, north of the Seelow Heights. However, unlike many other generals in the field, Manteuffel refused to be bullied by Hitler. During military conferences the general often stood up to him, and outlined the dire situation without glossing over the difficulties that plagued the front. Although Hitler's views were totally different to Manteuffel's, the Führer liked his transparency and admired his iron will and exceptional moral courage. He told Manteuffel that as an exceptional commander he would hold back the enemy. However, when the general toured the battlefield after taking command of his army, he later recalled, "The first impression that I gained of the army was downright depressing as it lacked virtually everything that was necessary for an effective defense." Although it was a "panzer army," it did not include a single panzer division.

(Bundesarchiv Bild 146-1976-143-21)

Despite Heinrici's gloomy prediction, he placed the 9th Army at the front, from the Finow Canal to Guben, including the Seelow Heights. Although the troops knew they were fighting an enemy that was almost ten times larger than them, many were infused with courage and the determination to continue the fight. Scores of these soldiers were emplaced along nothing more than lines of trenches with various tank obstacles and reinforced machine-gun and mortar pits. Each line of defense was mined and consisted of antitank strongpoints and a network of obstacles protected by extensive barbed-wire barriers. Manning these lines were well-dug-in soldiers armed with a collection of weapons, ranging from the standard Karabiner 98k bolt-action rifle, to captured Soviet weapons and the deadly Panzerfaust antitank launchers. Spaced out at intervals along the front were gun pits surrounded by antitank obstacles and lines of trenches with a collection of Pak and artillery guns, occasionally supplemented by diminishing numbers of 8.8 cm antiaircraft guns.

All these defenses were spread out to maximize the manpower available to bolster the defense of the Heights. Heinrici also ordered German engineers to flood the Oder floodplain, already boggy from the spring thaw. He thus turned the plain into swampland by releasing the water from a reservoir farther upstream. Digging in along the heights overlooking the Oder's muddy floodplain gave the defenders a tactical advantage, as Heinrici knew that the Red Army's heavy vehicles would be forced along the limited number of roads. This allowed the defenders to take a measure of advantage of the situation to afford them maximum use of their antitank and artillery weaponry to inflict maximum casualties.

In Profile:
General Hellmuth Reyman
November 24, 1892–December 8, 1988

On March 6, 1945, Reyman replaced General Bruno Ritter von Hauenschild as commander of what was known as the Berlin Defense Area. Prior to his appointment, the general had fought doggedly in Latvia commanding the 11th Infantry Division when his troops had been encircled and temporarily trapped in the Kurland Pocket. Four months later when he took command of the defense of Berlin, he found to his dismay there were no proper plans to resist an urbanized attack into the city. There was also no policy to evacuate the children and elderly from the capital either. It appeared that the Nazi government had failed to acknowledge that an attack into

the city was possible and had therefore almost ignored the possibility. Reyman, who was a great planner both in defensive and offensive operations, immediately set to work by preparing the city for an imminent attack, regardless of what the Nazi hierarchy was thinking. Weeks later as growing reports reached the Führerbunker that the Red Army was preparing its forces along the Seelow Heights, Hitler was preparing a scorched earth policy known as the "Nero Decree." Reyman was appalled by the order and lost all faith in the Nazi regime. As Soviet forces began preparing their positions for a direct assault into the city, the general urged the Führer to allow the underage civilian population of Berlin to be evacuated immediately. Hitler refused outright. Instead, the general urged all civilians to hide in cellars and basements and hold out through the coming battle.

German Order of Battle, February–April 1945

ARMY GROUP VISTULA (Heinrici)

9th Army (Busse)

Sturm Battalion AOK

Hitlerjugend Nahkampf Brigade

CI Corps (Berlin)

406th Volksartilleriekorps

111th Sturmgeschütz Lehr Brigade

Fallschirmjäger Panzerjäger Brigade Pirat

15th Schwereswerfer Regiment

53rd Flak Regiment

182nd Flak Regiment

16/69 Volkssturm Battalion

16/128 Volkssturm Battalion

4 Volkssturm Companies (16/75, 16/123, 16/511, 16/67/1)

5th Jäger Division

56th Jäger Regiment

75th Jäger Regiment

5th Jäger Artillery Regiment

606th Division Stab z.b.V.

Schatten Regiment A (I. & II. Battalions + 14. Company)

Regiment Sator (Battalions Bählkow, Gorny, & Spandau)

Regiment Rohrde (Battalion Potsdam & Alarm? Battalion 67)

Police Landschützen Battalion Bremen (606th Füsilier Battalion?)

606th Artillery Regiment

1606th Panzerjäger Company

3rd Panzer A. u. E. Battalion

309th Berlin Infantry Division

Wachregiment Gross Deutschland (I. & II. Battalions)

652nd Grenadier Regiment (I. & II. Battalions)

653rd Grenadier Regiment (I. & II. Battalions)

309th Artillery Regiment

309th Pioneer Battalion

309th Panzerjäger Battalion

1234th Fhj Regiment Potsdam (I. & II. Battalions)

16./1129th PanzerJägd Battalion

4 Volkssturm Battalion (Alarm Battalions Brandenburg, 323rd Potsdam, Spandau, 338th z.b.V.)

25th Panzergrenadier Division

35th Panzergrenadier Regiment (I.–III. Battalions)

119th Panzergrenadier Regiment (I.–III. Battalions)

5th Panzer Battalion

25th Pioneer Battalion

25th Panzerjäger Battalion

125th Reconnaissance Battalion

292nd Heeres Flak Battalion

25th Panzergrenadier Artillery Regiment

Kampfgruppe 1,001 Nights

LVI Panzer Corps (Weidling)

Heeres 920th StuG Lehr Brigade

9th Fallschirmjäger Division

25th 9th Fallschirmjäger Regiment (I. & III. Battalions)

26th 9th Fallschirmjäger Regiment (I. & III. Battalions)

9th Fallschirmjäger Regiment (I.–III. Battalions)

9th Fallschirmjäger Rocket Battalion

9th Fallschirmjäger Pioneer Battalion

18th Panzergrenadier Division

118th Panzer Battalion

30th Panzergrenadier Regiment (mot) (I.–III. Battalions)

51st Panzergrenadier Regiment (mot)

18th Artillery Regiment (mot) (I.–III. Battalions)

118th Reconnaissance Battalion

20th Panzergrenadier Division

8th Panzer Battalion

76th Panzergrenadier Regiment

90th Panzergrenadier Regiment

20th Artillery Regiment (part)

Müncheberg Panzer Division

Panzer Battalion Müncheberg

1st Panzergrenadier Regiment Müncheberg (I. & II. Battalions)

2nd Panzergrenadier Regiment Müncheberg (I. & II. Battalions)

Panzerjäger Company Müncheberg

Panzerpioneer Company Müncheberg

Artillery Regiment Müncheberg

XI SS Panzer Corps
(Kleinheisterkamp)

404th Volksartillerie Corps

1240th Fhj Regiment (I. & II. Battalions)

303rd Doberitz Infantry Division

300th Grenadier Regiment (I. & II. Battalions)

301st Grenadier Regiment (I. & II. Battalions)

302nd Grenadier Regiment (I. & II. Battalions)

303rd Artillery Regiment

303rd Füsilier Battalion

303rd Pioneer Battalion

303rd Panzerjäger Battalion

169th Infantry Division

378th Grenadier Regiment (I.–III. Battalions)

392nd Grenadier Regiment (I.–III. Battalions)

1242nd Fhj Regiment (I. & II. Battalions + 13. & 14. Companies)

230th Pioneer Battalion

230th Jagdpanzer Battalion

230th Artillery Regiment (I.–IV. Battalions)

Festungs Pak Verband XXVI

712th Infantry Division

Fhj Regiment 1239 (Wiener Neustadt) (I. & II. Battalions)

Fhj Regiment 1241 (Güstrow) (I. & II. Battalions)

Alarm Battalion Hauck

108th Volkssturm Battalion

Schatten Regiment B (part)

1712th Artillery Regiment

Kurmark Panzergrenadier Division

Panzer Battalion Kurmark

Panzergrenadier Regiment Kurmark (I. & II. Battalions)

Artillery Battalion Kurmark

Frankfurt an der Oder Garrison
(Biehler)

Festungs Grenadier Regiment 1

Festungs Grenadier Regiment 2

Festungs Grenadier Regiment 3

Festungs Grenadier Regiment 4

Festungs M.G. Battalion 84

Festungs KGr. 5

Festungs KGr. 6

Festungs KGr. 7

Festungs KGr. 8

Festungs Infantry Flak Battalion 829 (part)

Festungs Pioneer Sperr Battalion 952

Festungs Pak Verband XXVI

Heavy Flak Battalion 185

Heavy Flak Battalion 405

Festungs Artillery Stab 1320

Festungs Artillery Battalion 1,325

Festungs Artillery Battalion 1,326

Festungs Artillery Battalion 1,327

Panzer Jagd Battalion 2

V SS Mountain Corps (Jeckeln)

408th Volksartillerie Brigade

15th SS Panzerjäger Company

2nd Panzerjäger Battalion (part)

561st SS Panzerjäger Battalion

286th Infantry Division

Regiment von Petersdorf (part)

1237th Fhj Regiment (part)

Alarm Battalion Brieskow

27/151 Volkssturm Battalion Dresden

7/108 Volkssturm Battalion Mainfranken

Volkssturm Battalion Oberdonau

Verstärke Pioneer Battalion 275

32nd SS Grenadier Division

86th SS Grenadier Regiment (I. & II. Battalions)

87th SS Grenadier Regiment (I. & II. Battalions)

32nd SS Artillery Regiment

Volkssturm Battalion Thüringen

391st Security Division

1233rd Fhj Grenadier Regiment (I.–III. Battalions)

95th Grenadier Regiment (I. & II. Battalions)

239th Sicherungs Battalion

Pioneer Battalion (part)

SS Sturm Battalion z.v.B.

8/16 Volkssturm Battalion

Rägener Division

SS Verband Fhr Schüle Arolsen (I.–III. Battalions)

Police Battalion Döring (incl. 286th Security Division)

Reserve

156th Infantry Division

1313th Grenadier Regiment (I. to III. Battalions)

1314th Grenadier Regiment (I. to III. Battalions)

1315th Grenadier Regiment (I. to III. Battalions)

1456th Artillery Regiment (I. & II. Battalions)

1456th Pioneer Battalion

ARMY GROUP CENTER (Schörner)

4th Panzer Army (Graser)

V Corps (Wäger)

35th SS Police Grenadier Division

69th SS and Police Grenadier Regiment

70th SS and Police Grenadier Regiment

71st SS and Police Grenadier Regiment

35th SS and Police Füsilier Battalion

35th SS Artillery Regiment

29th SS Polizei-Schützen Regiment

30th SS Polizei Schutzen Regiment

Ausbildung Regiment 561

Corps MG Battalion 95

Alarm Regiment 94

Alarm Regiment 97

Panzerjäger Battalion 4

681st Heavy Anti-Tank Battalion

1244th Fj Regiment (I. & II. Battalions)

72nd Waffen-SS Grenadier Regiment

73rd Waffen-SS Grenadier Regiment

36th Fusilier Company

36th SS Artillery Battalion

Tank Battalion Standort 1

275th Infantry Division

342nd Infantry Division

21st Panzer Division

12th Army (Wenck)

XX Corps (Koehler)

Theodor Körner RAD Infantry Division

Ulrich von Hutten Infantry Division

Ferdinand von Schill Infantry Division

Scharnhorst Infantry Division

XXXIX Panzer Corps (Arndt)

Clausewitz Panzer Division

Under OKW to April 21

Schlageter RAD Division

84th Infantry Division

Clausewitz Panzer Division

Under 12th Army April 21–26

84th Infantry Division

324th Hamburg Reserve Infantry Division

588th Grenadier Regiment (I. & II. Battalions)

589th Grenadier Regiment (I. & II. Battalions)

324th Artillery Regiment (I. & II. Battalions)

324th Fusilier Battalion

Meyer Infantry Division

Möller Infantry Regiment

Heising Infantry Regiment

XXXXI Panzer Corps (Holste)

Von Hake Infantry Division

1st Von Hake Grenadier Regiment

2nd Von Hake Grenadier Regiment

199th Infantry Division

V-Weapons Infantry Division

901st z.b.V Artillery Regiment

XLVIII Panzer Corps (von Edelsheim)

14th Flak Division

90th Flak Regiment

121st Heavy Flak Battalion

568th Heavy Flak Battalion

729th Light Flak Battalion

43/IV Homeland Flak Battalion

120th Flak Regiment

307th Heavy Flak Battalion

323rd Heavy Flak Battalion

357th Heavy Flak Battalion

662nd Heavy Flak Battalion

525th E heavy Flak Battalion

80/XIII Homeland Flak Battalion

140th Flak Regiment

432nd Heavy Flak Battalion

722nd Light Flak Battalion

728th Light Flak Battalion

664th Light Flak Battalion

19th Flak Battalion

73rd Searchlight Regiment

199th Searchlight Battalion

258th Searchlight Battalion

328th Searchlight Battalion

367th Searchlight Battalion

500th Searchlight Battalion

510th Searchlight Battalion

134th Luftnachrichten Battalion

Kampfgruppe Leipzig (Volkssturm Battalions Leipzig)

Kampfgruppe Halle (8 Volkssturm Battalions + 1 Ersatz Battalion)

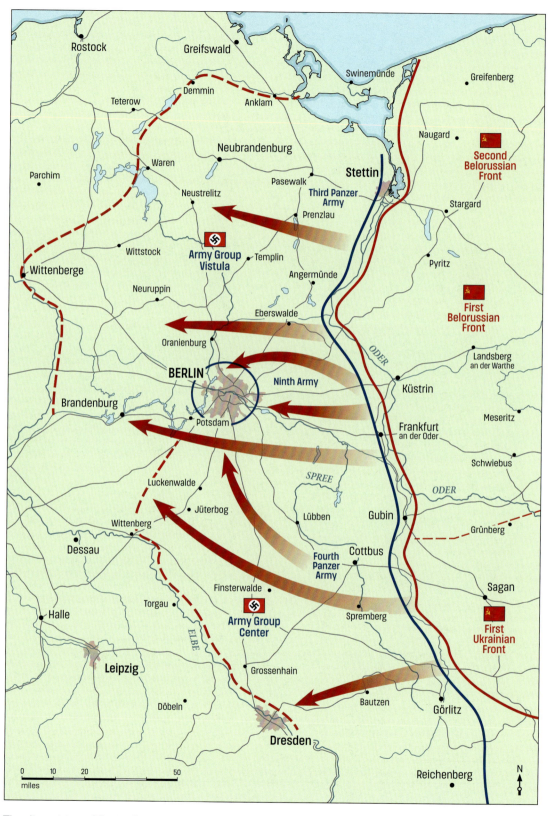

The disposition of Soviet forces advancing towards Berlin, March 1945.

Soviet Preparations

By the end of March 1945, Soviet plans for the Berlin strategic offensive operation had been worked out by the Stavka, with the commanders of the 1st and 2nd Belorussian and 1st Ukrainian Fronts, as well their Chiefs of Staff. On March 31, as Red Army troops drew up along the east bank of the Oder, the Stavka coordinated the final plans and details for the operation against Berlin. Stalin made it clear to his commanders that Berlin should be taken as quickly as possible, and the timetable for preparing the operation was limited. It was necessary, he said, to begin no later than April 16 and complete the whole operation within two weeks. Initially, none of the fronts was given the ultimate objective of capturing the capital. Stalin told his commanders, "Whoever breaks in first, let him take Berlin."

On April 2 a directive was issued to the commander of the 1st Ukrainian Front, Marshal Ivan S. Konev, who was moving slowly in the south. He was ordered to advance in the Cottbus area and south of Berlin and annihilate enemy positions there; this was to be completed no later than the tenth–twelfth day of the operation, reaching the Beelitz–Wittenberg line, and then along the Elbe as far as Dresden. The front's main attack, 35 miles south of Berlin, was planned along the Spremberg–Beelitz axis. The 3rd and 4th Guards Tank Armies were to be committed to support the infantry's drive in the area south of the capital. Initially, it was thought that after this success the 1st Ukrainian Front would swing north and move directly on Berlin.

An ISU-122S belonging to the 3rd Belorussian Front following the capture of Königsberg in early April 1945.

A Soviet tank crew servicing their ISU-122, changing the tracks of the vehicle.

In Profile:
Marshal Georgy Zhukov
December 1, 1896–June 18, 1974

Zhukov was probably one of the most important commanders in the Red Army at the pinnacle of the Berlin strategic offensive operation in April 1945. As a commander, he was regarded as decisive and firm. He was disciplined, stubborn, and persistent, and was respected by his men. In 1941 he organized the defense of Leningrad and was appointed defender of Moscow the same year. He oversaw the defense of Stalingrad and was primarily responsible for the success of the battle of Kursk in 1943. In March 1944 he was appointed commander of the 1st Ukrainian Front, where he successfully led a Soviet offensive through Belorussia which consequently saw the collapse of German Army Group Center. On November 16, 1945, he was appointed commander of the 1st Belorussian Front where he planned and executed the Vistula–Oder offensive. In March 1945, Stalin gave Zhukov full responsibility for coordinating operations against Berlin.

A column of T-34-85 tanks advancing through a forest in late February 1945, preparing for their assault against Berlin.

On April 6 a directive was issued to the 2nd Belorussian Front, which was not to take a direct part in the capture of Berlin but was given the task to attack to the northwest, cross the Oder north of Schwedt, and strike toward Neustrelitz. Its thrust was intended to drive the defending 3rd Panzer Army back against the coast and cover the advance toward Berlin in the north.

On April 9, after a long resistance, Königsberg in East Prussia finally fell to Soviet forces. This allowed formations of the 2nd Belorussian Front to move freely westward and advance to the east bank of the Oder River. By mid-April the 2nd Belorussian Front had successfully pushed back the 3rd Panzer Army and had taken a bridgehead 10 miles long above the city of Stettin, which had been turned into a fortress and was being defended by Fortress Division Stettin. It was formed from elements of the 3rd Panzer Army and was to put up a dogged defense. While the battle of Stettin raged, remaining units and formations of the 2nd Belorussian Front bypassed the city and attacked German defensive positions north of Berlin.

South of the 2nd Belorussian Front, the 1st Belorussian Front had moved its boundary from the Baltic coast down toward the town of Schwedt on the Oder. Its forces (comprising five armies, including the 1st and 2nd Guards Tank Armies) were moving southwestward into position for a frontal attack toward Berlin out of the Küstrin bridgehead. East of the capital, powerful armored units began making wide sweeping movements north and south to support an encirclement of Berlin with the two other fronts.

Concealed inside a forest, a T-34-85 tank crew services their tank prior to operations against the Seelow Heights. Note other tanks also parked in the forest.

In Profile:
Soviet Soldiers with PPSh-41s

Soviet Soldier, 12th Guards Rifle Corps, 3rd Shock Army, Oder River, April 1945. (Renato Dalmaso)

A decorated Soviet soldier armed with the PPSh-41 (Shpagin's machine pistol 41). He wears the RKKA Soviet army tunic and side cap, or *pilotka*, complete with stitched red star.

Soviet NCO, 32nd Guards Rifle Corps, 5th Guards Army, Oder River, April 1945. (Renato Dalmaso)

A senior NCO armed with the PPSh-41 smokes a cigarette. He wears the RKKA Soviet army tunic and side cap, or *pilotka*, complete with stitched red star. Just above his right pocket flap he wears the Order of the Red Star.

A crew of a T-34-85 in a forest prior to the commencement of operations against Berlin in early April 1945.

Pulling up into a surrounding forest, Soviet T-34-85 tanks and ISU-122 assault guns prepare for operations against the Seelow Heights.

ISU-122 heavy self-propelled assault guns in a forest.

31

Farther south, the 1st Ukrainian Front—which had encircled and destroyed more than five German divisions in Upper Silesia and pushed back the remnants of German forces defending the area into the Sudeten Mountains—was now veering north to support the encirclement of Berlin. The 1st Ukrainian Front planned two major drives: one by the 3rd and 4th Guards Tank Armies with three infantry armies to cross the Neisse between Forst and Muskau and to push its formations northwest; the other to be undertaken by two armies, from north of Görlitz to Dresden. The main focal point of the attack was given to Zhukov's 1st Belorussian Front. The 1st Belorussian Front had successfully moved along the Oder River from Frankfurt an der Oder in the south to the Baltic; it was now moving into an area in front of the Seelow Heights in the center of the front directly east of Berlin to prepare to attack the capital, as ordered by Stalin.

Prior to the operation, the 1st Belorussian Front launched several reconnaissance missions over a two-day period throughout April 14–15 to ascertain the Germans' main defensive zone. By launching the reconnaissance actions along the Oder in the region of the Seelow Heights, it fooled the German command into thinking it was the main attack. As a result, several German units that had dug in were redeployed, leaving them vulnerable. As for the Soviets, the reconnaissance mission was successful, and units were able to relay information to the artillery batteries to prepare their guns on specific sectors of the German front.

During the evening of April 15, long columns of Soviet vehicles, guns, and men of the 1st Belorussian Front finally moved to their assembly areas. The entire area was full of vehicles, artillery, and tanks. Concealed under trees and camouflage netting stood hundreds of antiaircraft and antitank guns, rocket launchers, tanks, tank destroyers, and armored vehicles, all waiting in preparation for the massive artillery bombardment. In total were some 908,000 troops, 3,155 tanks and armored vehicles, 16,934 guns, and over 7,000,000 rounds of artillery ammunition in preparation for the offensive.

In Profile:
Marshal Ivan S. Konev
December 28, 1897–May 21, 1973

Konev was one of the most famous Red Army commanders. He took part in the build-up of operations against Berlin and eventually supported some of the main attacks on the city. Officially though, he was subordinate to Zhukov, and therefore during the latter part of the war became his main rival. In fact, Konev attempted to get authorization from Stalin to have his 1st Ukrainian Front capture Berlin, but Stalin gave that honor to Zhukov, much to Konev's disappointment. However, despite this Konev's front went on to capture several key military targets, including Prague, and he had the final honor when he was asked to get involved in the capture of Berlin when Zhukov's forces were unable to overcome solid resistance.

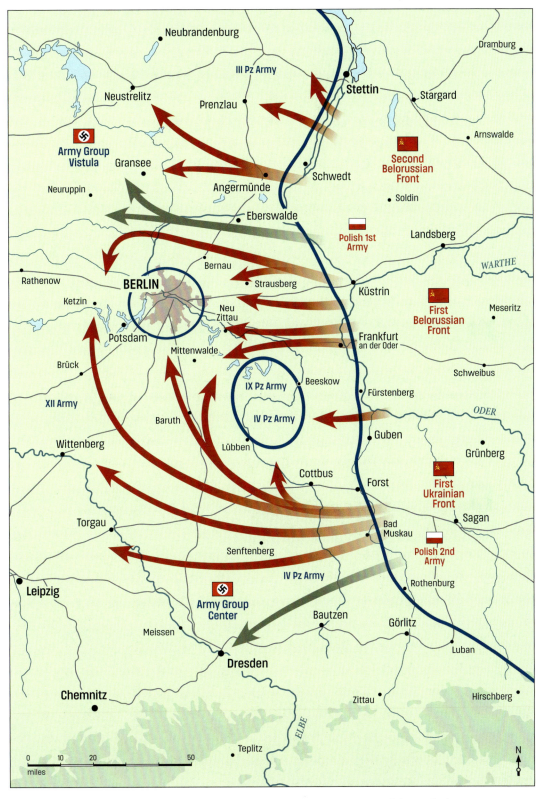

The disposition of Red Army and Polish forces advancing from the River Oder with the objective of encircling Berlin.

Phase 1: Seelow–Berlin Offensive Operation, April 16–19

The Seelow Heights are situated around the town of Seelow some 56 miles east of Berlin, and overlook the Oderbruch, the stream that flows through the western floodplain of the River Oder, which is a further 12 miles to the east. The Heights were regarded by German and Soviet soldiers as the "Gates to Berlin," because the main eastern route out of Berlin runs through them. They were pivotal to the success of the whole Soviet offensive operation against the capital, and a matter of life and death to the Germans defending it.

The main strategic focus of the Soviet assault against the Seelow Heights was a horseshoe-shaped plateau between 100 and 200 feet in height. It was here at Seelow on April 15, 1945, that German intelligence began forewarning of an imminent Soviet attack. Hitler bluntly told Heinrici that General Theodor Busse's troops of the 9th Army should conduct an effective resistance in the face of overwhelming firepower; if the general could hold the Red Army back, then this would thwart the enemy from using the Seelow Heights as a springboard into

Soviet artillery bombards German positions during the battle for the Seelow Heights.

A battery of 122 mm howitzer M1938s (M-30s) soften up German positions. These weapons were a divisional-level howitzer; each rifle division had two artillery regiments which included two batteries of these guns.

A well-placed and well-concealed battery of heavy 152 mm howitzer-gun M1937s (ML-20s) on the edge of a forest in preparation for a fire mission.

Foliage has been attached to the front of this 152 mm howitzer-gun M1937 (ML-20s). These weapons were primarily used for indirect fire against enemy positions such as field fortifications and key objects in the rear.

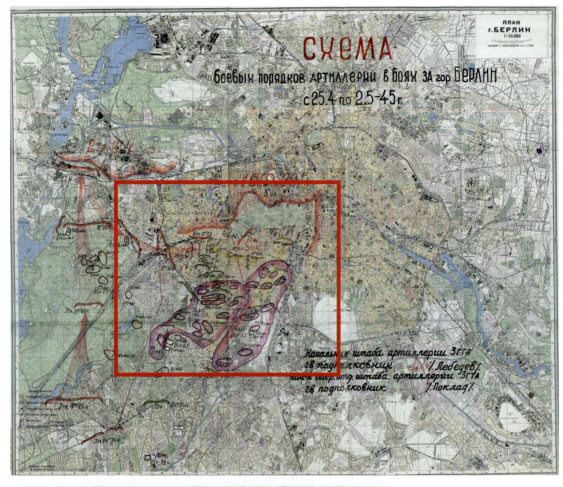

Two Russian maps showing the disposition of Red Army forces during the battle of Berlin in April 1945.

the suburbs of Berlin. Hitler made it clear that holding every defensive position would mean that the enemy could be sucked into a longer battle of attrition. However, Heinrici knew that the Führer's strategy was purely prolonging the inevitable battle of Berlin.

Defending the Heights was the 9th Army, comprised of 14 divisions and part of Fortress (*Festung*) Frankfurt. These divisions were dug in along defensive lines between the Finow Canal and Guben. Farther south, the front was held grimly by what was left of the 4th Panzer Army, which was facing the 1st Ukrainian Front along defenses strung out along the Lusatian Neisse River between Görlitz and Guben.

In the early hours of April 16, German intelligence was monitoring increased Soviet activity as German troops prepared their final defensive positions. Along the Oder floodplain, Flak and Pak guns had been installed as well as various trenches, antitank ditches, and bunkers comprising a motley array of mortar and machine-gun crews. These lines of defense were supported by 587 tanks and self-propelled guns and 2,625 artillery pieces, including some 695 antiaircraft guns. Some 143 antiaircraft searchlights had been placed along the front line, too, to blind the enemy. Three main defensive belts had been constructed known as the Hauptkampflinie (Front Line), Hardenberg-Stellung, and Wotan-Stellung. These formidable defenses stretched back 10–15 miles.

In front of these defensive belts, Zhukov's 1st Belorussian Front was stacked back mile after mile, supported by thousands of Katyusha rocket launchers and artillery pieces that were being readied for the opening barrage. With almost a million Soviet soldiers—including some 78,000 soldiers of the Communist Polish 1st Army—these forces were distributed among nine regular and two tank armies comprising seventy-seven rifle divisions, two cavalry, two mechanized and five powerful tank corps, eight artillery and one mortar division, including various rocket launcher and artillery brigades. The front boasted some 3,000 tanks and self-propelled guns, including 18,000 artillery pieces and mortars.

Zhukov's mighty force had 11 armies dug in along the Oder between Schwedt and the Finow Canal, including the 61st Army and the 1st Polish Army. Alongside these units, at Küstrin was the 47th Army, 3rd and 5th Shock Armies, and the 8th Guards Army. From

A Soviet photograph depicting the battle of the Seelow Heights. Here a mortar crew is embroiled in action; one of their wounded comrades is being assisted by a medic.

A German forward observation post on the Seelow Heights. A soldier appears to be trying to deduce the location of the enemy.

A forward position on the Seelow Heights, April 1945. A soldier is in his trench, his kit and mess tins next to him.

A Luftwaffe 8.8 cm Flak gun being used against ground targets on the Seelow Heights.

A Volkssturm light MG 42 crew move to another position during heavy fighting.

the river line south of Guben were the 69th Army and 33rd Army. The 1st Guards and 2nd Guards Tank Armies (including the 3rd Army) were in reserve. As Zhukov's troops completed their battle positions, there was a general feeling among them— not of jubilation at launching the greatest attack so far on the Eastern Front, but an ardent belief in duty to the Motherland, and the duty to finally crush Nazism forever.

At 03:00, the stillness of the night was suddenly broken by shouts of Soviet officers ordering their gunners to begin one of the largest artillery bombardments of the war. Some 9,000 Soviet guns firing 500,000 shells simultaneously opened fire against Busse's forces. The massive bombardment raged for almost 30 minutes. However, the ground Zhukov's forces occupied was boggy from the spring thaw, and this was exacerbated by the fact that German engineers had released water from the reservoir upstream that had turned the plain into a swamp. Consequently, this made movement difficult for the Soviet armor, slowing their advance. Another hindrance was that Heinrici had tactically withdrawn the bulk of his men from the first belt of defense to the second, which had saved many soldiers from being annihilated in the opening Red Army bombardment.

Soviet soldiers had to wade through the boggy plain with German gunners raining down their own fire on the attackers, causing massive losses. Surprised by the solid enemy defense, Zhukov quickly ordered high-powered antiaircraft searchlights to illuminate the Heights so that his infantry could advance. However, this only made them easier to target as they crawled through the swamp. Undeterred, Soviet artillery batteries poured a storm of fire onto the German positions. In some sectors of the front the noise was stupefying; it left several soldiers bleeding from the ears.

By the end of the first day of the attack, Zhukov's gunners had fired over 1,250,000 rounds. But his forces had only managed to advance some six miles, capturing the villages of Sachsendorf and Trebbin. The 1st Polish Army had crossed the Oder near Güstebiese, but had ground to a halt in the face of stiff resistance. Only the first line of defensive fortifications had been captured, and this with heavy losses. Zhukov was under pressure from Stalin to take the Seelow Heights at all costs and quickly.

A typical German defensive position on the Seelow Heights with soldiers in their foxholes armed with Panzerfausts.

A Soviet convoy passes German vehicles destroyed during the fighting on the Seelow Heights, including a Tiger II tank which appears to have been abandoned by the crew. A knocked-out Tiger I can also be seen. Frightened horses have broken from their harnesses and are struggling in the ditch.

A knocked-out Tiger I tank belonging to the 502nd Heavy Panzer Battalion at Seelow Heights. Due to the lack of Tiger IIs, the battalion was issued with a mixture of Tiger Is, Tiger IIs, and Jagdpanzer 38s (Hetzer) tank destroyers. The battalion was disbanded on April 27, 1945, following massive losses.

German troops inflicted heavy losses on Soviet forces in the Seelow Heights. Pictured here are infantry and *panzertruppen* in a destroyed village east of Berlin. A knocked-out Soviet ISU-122 is surrounded by its dead crew. This vehicle was a powerful assault gun, but it was often used it as a self-propelled howitzer or a long-range tank destroyer.

The next day, April 17, the Soviet 1st and 2nd Guards Tank Armies were committed to the battle, but due to heavy traffic congestion at the bridgeheads many of the armored units were not able to make any contribution to the offensive. Instead, another heavy artillery bombardment was launched against the Seelow Heights and by nightfall the Stein-Stellung line was breached by advanced elements of the 5th Shock Army and the 2nd Guards Tank Army. The 4th Guards Rifle Corps of the 8th Guards Army, supported by units of the 11th Guards Tank Corps of the 1st Guards Tank Army, then broke through the German defenses on the right flank and made deep penetrating advances.

As the second line of German defenses was breached, farther south Konev's 1st Ukrainian Front was ordered to attack the 4th Panzer Army between Görlitz and Guben. Unlike Zhukov, Konev laid a smokescreen across the battlefield instead of illuminating it with searchlights. This confused the Germans as to the exact location of the attacks. Konev also used the tactic of preselecting targets instead of saturating large areas with artillery fire. This enabled troops to use blasted paths where they could assault enemy lines in support of tanks. Within hours of the initial attacks, Konev's forces had crossed the Neisse River at numerous places; he planned to drive his armored spearheads toward Berlin. Although Konev had not been tasked to take Berlin, the operation to the south put additional pressure on the German defense at Seelow Heights and allowed his archrival Zhukov to take more ground.

By April 19 the 1st Belorussian Front was continuing to advance, despite heavy losses. Although the Germans continued to put up dogged resistance, the defensive lines began to crumble. Numerous counterattacks from German reserves of the 11th SS Panzergrenadier Division Nordland, 23rd SS Panzergrenadier Division Nederland, and SS-Panzer Abteilung 103 were conducted, but Zhukov's troops had reached the third line of German defenses. Throughout the day the German lines were reduced to blasted rubble and those soldiers not encircled and killed retreated in panic and disorder along the Berlin highway back toward the suburbs of the capital.

In the final battles that ensued in and around the Seelow Heights, the 1st Belorussian and 1st Ukrainian Front simultaneously enveloped the remnants of the 9th Army and the 4th Panzer Army that had not escaped. With the collapse of these forces, for all intents and purposes, the German Eastern Front no longer existed. All that remained of troops fighting east of Berlin were a few isolated pockets.

A Soviet soldier using dogs to pull supplies through a destroyed German town east of Berlin, April 1945.

Phase 2: Stettin–Rostock Offensive Operation, April 16–May 5

Part of the second phase of preparations for the battle of Berlin was another sub-offensive operation which coincided with attacks against the Seelow Heights. The plan was for the 2nd Belorussian Front to smash through enemy defenses along the Oder and deprive the German 3rd Panzer Army of movement toward the defense of Berlin. In February 1945, the 3rd Panzer Army was one of the principal armies in the new Army Group Vistula. On March 10, General Hasso von Manteuffel became commander of the army, which had been ordered to dig in along the River Oder and defend positions north of the Seelow Heights, to block Red Army formations and units moving toward Eastern Pomerania and Berlin.

In front of the 3rd Panzer Army was the 2nd Belorussian Front, which had moved into the Stettin–Schwedt sector. It comprised three powerful armies—the 65th, 70th, and 49th—supported by three tank armies—the 1st, 3rd, and 8th—plus the 8th Mechanized and 3rd Cavalry Corps. Its main objective was to break through German defenses in the area and develop an offensive toward Neustrelitz. Once this had been completed, the armies would then drive on to the Demmin–Malkhin–Warren–Wittenberg line. On the right wing of the front, the 2nd Shock and 19th Armies were ordered to force a breakthrough of German defenses east and west of the Oder. Once this had been achieved, mobile units were to advance at speed and quickly develop an offensive in the western and northwestern directions of the front. This operation was planned to cut off the 3rd Panzer Army from Berlin and annihilate the remaining elements of all enemy forces in the region north of the Berlin and the Baltic coast. Once this operation had been successfully completed, the 2nd Belorussian Front—supported by units of the 1st Belorussian Front—would maneuver in wide sweeping thrusts and encircle Berlin from the north.

An ISS-122 assault gun which still has its winter camouflage paint.

An ISS-122 halted inside a town.

A column of T-34-85s halted along a road during the advance to the Oder, April 1945.

Fighting at the Oder was fierce with the 3rd Panzer Army putting up bitter resistance. Soviet riflemen next to a T-34 tank warily check out an enemy strongpoint.

43

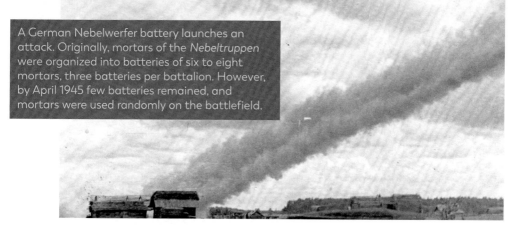

A German Nebelwerfer battery launches an attack. Originally, mortars of the *Nebeltruppen* were organized into batteries of six to eight mortars, three batteries per battalion. However, by April 1945 few batteries remained, and mortars were used randomly on the battlefield.

Just prior to the second phase of the operation, the 2nd Belorussian Front regrouped its forces along a 100-mile front stretching from the Baltic Sea to Schwedt. It had just completed its East Pomeranian offensive operation and needed resupply to begin a new offensive. Over a period of seven to ten days prior to the offensive, the 2nd Belorussian Front consolidated, having marched some 280 miles. Armored vehicles, artillery, and supplies were transported by rail, while most of the infantry moved by road. When the front arrived along the Oder it quickly reorganized in preparation for attack.

On April 16, artillery units launched a massive artillery barrage to pave a path through enemy defenses and reach the east bank of the Oder. This barrage began with reconnaissance units probing German positions, followed by the first divisional echelons crashing into action across the river. By the morning of April 18, the whole strike force was embroiled in the offensive, advancing over the Oder. Although movement was severely hampered by the boggy terrain, the advance persisted.

The next day Red Army troops continued their clearing operation along the Oder, despite heavy resistance from German artillery. For the next two days fighting was intense, as both sides fought from one fixed position to another. The Germans tried to hold their positions, while the Soviets used air and ground bombardments to gain more ground. Within two days, on April 22, the 2nd Belorussian Front had secured a bridgehead on the west bank of the Oder over 10 miles deep and was heavily embroiled in fighting determined formations of the 3rd Panzer Army. Fighting raged day and night, but within three days the 2nd Belorussian Front had successfully broken through the German lines around the bridgehead at Stettin. The city was heavily defended by elements of the 10th SS Panzer Division. Little fighting had occurred in the area until the Soviets widened their bridgeheads between Greifenhagen and Stettin. On April 24, the Red Army was in full attack near Schwedt, and once again widened their bridgeheads between Gartz and Stettin. The next day, supported by massive artillery bombardments and ground-attack aircraft, Soviet forces advanced from their Gartz bridgehead to the west of Tantow and Kasekow.

Throughout the morning of April 26 fighting intensified around the southern outskirts of Stettin. Later that day the city fell and advanced echelons of the 2nd Belorussian Front drove west toward Prenzlau, forcing the center of the 3rd Panzer Army back. On April 27

A column of IS-2 tanks.

A Volkssturm mortar crew in action between Gartz and Stettin. They all wear civilian garb.

Two Wehrmacht soldiers in a trench armed with the standard German infantry Karabiner 98k bolt-action rifle, Stg24 stick grenades at the ready.

An ISU-152 has been knocked out trying to break through a line of German trenches northwest of Berlin.

45

A Heer mortar crew using a halftrack personnel carrier to launch their attacks.

A German 8.8 cm Flak gun being used in a ground role defending a bridge northwest of Berlin.

German soldiers inside a burning town following heavy fighting.

Red Army troops aboard a T-34-85 tank deploy into battle.

Soviet soldiers pose with two captured German weapons: left the 7.92 mm Gewehr 43 rifle, center MP 40 submachine gun, and on the right a soldier holds the Soviet PPD-40 submachine gun.

Prenzlau was captured along with the town of Angermünde 45 miles northwest of Berlin. With these areas secured, Red Army formations then advanced to the Baltic city of Rostock to prevent German forces there from moving in the direction of Berlin. What followed over the next few days was bitter fighting, with the Soviets containing the 3rd Panzer Army. Fighting north of the German capital was fierce, but by early May the Red Army had destroyed 18 German divisions, including one tank and two motorized, three combat groups, and several brigades, regiments, and battalions.

During the offensive, the Soviets had successfully advanced westward, covering some 180 miles. The operation had cleared, destroyed, or contained enemy formations in northwestern Pomerania as well as most of Mecklenburg and Brandenburg, but most importantly, it had stopped the 3rd Panzer Army from taking part in the defense of Berlin. The success of the operation meant that the 2nd Belorussian Front could now move freely west toward the British 21st Army Group, and advance north to finally secure and capture the Baltic ports of Stralsund and Rostock.

Soviet troops in Stettin. On April 26, the 65th Army stormed Stettin and broke through the German defenses on the Randov River.

In Profile:
Soviet Tanker and ROK Flamethrower Soldier

Soviet Tanker, 107th Tank Brigade, 16th Tank Corps, 2nd Guards Tank Army, Seelow Heights, April 1945. (Renato Dalmaso)

This Soviet tanker wears the familiar tankman's helmet, complete with jacket, over his army tunic. He also wears a black leather belt with star buckle. Likely secured to the belt is a sidearm holster with the Nagant M1895 revolver.

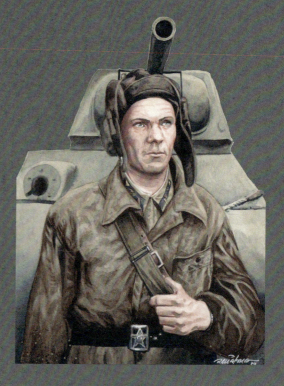

Portable ROK Flamethrower Soldier, 28th Guards Rifle Corps, 8th Guards Army, Seelow Heights, April 1945. (Renato Dalmaso)

This soldier is armed with the ROK man-portable flamethrower. He wears the Soviet *ushanka* (winter hat) and the *telogreika* (cottonwool-padded jacket) over his standard infantryman's tunic.

Phase 3: Cottbus–Potsdam Offensive Operation, April 16–27

The Cottbus–Potsdam offensive operation was the third of the five sub-operations that were part of the Berlin Strategic offensive operation. The objective was for the 1st Ukrainian Front to destroy German positions in the Cottbus region and to the area south of Berlin, and to capture the line between Beelitz and Wittenberg and then spearhead its formations farther along the Elbe to Dresden. Its divisions were also to support operations to capture Berlin from the south, while simultaneously using its powerful forces to advance on Leipzig and deliver a crushing blow to the enemy in the general direction of Spremberg and Belzig.

Although the 1st Ukrainian Front was not involved in the plan to capture Berlin, Konev did draw up his own preparations for his army's participation in the battle for the capital. However, his main task was to break through the German defense on the western bank of the Neisse River in the region around Forst, where he was tasked with annihilating the enemy to the southeast of Klein Bademeisel. After destroying the German defense there, he was to rapidly develop the main offensive, bypass Cottbus from the south, and push forward at

ISU-122s of the 3rd Guards Tank Army move through a forest with the objective of crossing the Neisse River.

A Soviet mortar crew in action. According to Red Army reports, Cottbus had two defensive rings with a network of trenches protected by several German 7.5 cm Pak guns.

speed to reach the Zossen–Nimchek line via Belsitz. From here Konev's forces would be able to attack the capital from the south and southwest.

During the planning of the offensive there was a slight modification to direct the main assault straight through Cottbus. It was here that the Soviets wanted to inflict the main blow on the enemy. The 3rd Guards Tank Army, which was given a decisive role in the operation, was to cross the Neisse River supported by infantry formations, and then drive at speed and seize bridgeheads across the Spree River.

Opposing Konev's force were elements of Army Group Center under the brutal command of Field Marshal Ferdinand Schörner. Dug in along the battered lines on the Neisse River was the German V Corps comprising the 342nd Division, 214th Division, and the 375th Division, supported by a *Kampfgruppe* of Waffen-SS troops. This battle group contained the 35th SS Polizei Grenadierdivision and the 36th Waffen-SS Grenadierdivision supported by the Panzer Corps Grossdeutschland Brandenburg, Division 464, Divison zbV 615, and battle group of the 545th Volksgrenadierdivision.

Prior to the offensive, on April 15, Konev had ordered several probing attacks along the river to ascertain enemy strength. Almost immediately, Red Army units encountered a solid, well-organized defense. However, during these encounters the Germans were ordered to withdraw from their forward defense lines and fall back to their second line of trenches.

At dawn the following morning (April 16), Konev launched his offensive with a customary heavy preliminary artillery bombardment against the river line. Within an hour of the artillery attack, boats were brought up and an infantry crossing ensued. Almost immediately following a wave of heavy assaults, Soviet infantry seized bridgeheads on the

A Soviet rifleman surveys the damage to a knocked-out German 7.5 cm Pak 40-2 Marder II.

A young German Flak crew man their weapon in the Cottbus–Spremburg–Lauban area. Four Panzer divisions had been moved to the area, which included the Herman Göring Panzer and 20th Panzer Divisions.

A member of the Volkssturm and a Hitlerjugend boy soldier prepare to move to the front.

A Soviet mortar crew in action.

A Sturmgeschütz III Ausf. G out of action. It appears to have plowed into its final resting place.

Two Volkssturm soldiers killed in the Cottbus region, April 1945.

west bank. Pontoon bridges were then erected to allow the heavy armor and support vehicles to cross.

The 3rd Guards Army's 149th Division then advanced at breakneck speed from the southeast in Forst, where the Germans had built a line of defenses. Within hours of the attack, fighting raged inside the town with German troops ordered to fight to the last man or face execution. While Forst was engulfed in flame and smoke, the leading echelons of the 3rd Guards Tank Army skirted the town and attacked toward Domsdorf and Gross Schacksdorf.

Meanwhile, on the left flank of the 3rd Guards Tank Army, the 5th Guards Army was attacking the German bridgehead on the eastern bank of the Neisse River. Defending this part of the river was the 21st Panzer Division, which had been rushing its forces from Breslau toward Berlin. Supporting the division was the Führer-Begliet Division, which was advancing toward Spremberg, and the 10th SS Panzer Division Frundsberg, which was strung out between Cottbus and Spremberg.

German resistance was particularly determined despite the lack of ammunition and fuel. On April 17, to Konev's surprise, the Germans launched a counterattack toward the southern perimeter of Forst but were immediately repulsed. During the day fighting continued to rage with unabated ferocity as Soviet formations began an encircling operation around Forst. The 3rd Guards Army then made a series of attacks and stormed Forst.

As German defenses inside Forst crumbled, the 3rd Guards Tank Army captured Zimmersdorf and then drove west against the 21st Panzer Division. Despite German

A light MG 42 machine gun position in front of a town.

A German soldier armed with a captured Soviet PPSh-41 submachine gun moves stealthily along one of the numerous trenches the Cottbus–Spremburg area. Red Army aircraft carried out 1,813 sorties on April 16 alone to destroy enemy defenses.

counterattacks the panzer division was repulsed. As a result, parts of the front collapsed, which allowed the 4th Guards Tank Army time to seize bridgeheads to the north and south of Spremberg. With Spremberg threatened, the 4th Panzer Army was rushed to the sector between Cottbus and Spremberg and immediately counterattacked. Fighting raged for hours, but the Germans could not contain the Red Army. Spremberg was then bypassed from the north and south by the 4th Guards Tank Army to reach the Spree River.

Within four days of the offensive, the Soviets had managed to overcome the entire depth of the German defense on the Neisse River. Schörner's men lacked the reserves, armor, ammunition, and fuel needed to counterattack. The path to Berlin was wide open. Konev's forces continued to batter the Germans into submission and fight for Cottbus, while two tank armies advanced in the direction of the capital. German forces were immediately ordered to assist in the defense of Cottbus. Units of the 36th Waffen-SS Grenadier Division, the 242nd, 214th, and 275th Divisions, the 21st Panzer Division, and the reconnaissance battalion of the 10th SS Panzer Division Frundsberg, were all put into line to defend what Schörner called the last bastion of defense before Berlin. However, Soviet forces overwhelmed the German positions around the town; by the end of April 21, the Cottbus area was surrounded on its eastern, southern, and western entrances. This only left the northern approaches open for troops to escape: the alternative was total annihilation. On the afternoon of April 22 the town was captured, which allowed advanced Soviet formations to thunder north and exploit the region toward the Spree River.

A German MG 42 machine gunner tucks into a slice of bread.

A stationary column of T-34-85s awaits orders to begin their drive.

The next day a lull in the fighting allowed the 3rd Guards Tank Army to regroup before it resumed operations against Berlin. On the same day the 4th Guards Tank Army reached the Teltow Canal near Stahnsdorf and then halted before it outstripped its supply lines.

By April 25 the situation for the German forces defending positions in front of the 1st Ukrainian Front was dire. Konev's tank armies had effectively sealed the fate of the enemy in the southwestern sector of Berlin. With Cottbus surrounded and large areas south of the capital captured, the 3rd Guards Tank Army began attacking Berlin, while the 4th Guards Tank Army continued fighting for crossings over the Havel River southeast of Potsdam. Konev's main objective now was to seal Potsdam's fate. Potsdam is situated on the Havel River, downstream from Berlin within the city limits. Soviet formations were now bearing down on Potsdam; its capture would complete the encirclement of Berlin.

On April 25, the 6th Guards Mechanized Corps managed to cross the Havel and linkup with units of the 328th Division of the 47th Army, 1st Belorussian Front, thus completing the final encirclement of Berlin from the west. Within two days the 4th Guards Tank Army and the 47th Army were fighting in the Potsdam area before successfully securing the region, much to Stalin's jubilation. The Cottbus–Potsdam offensive operation was now completed, and this allowed Konev to push west and drive Busse's 9th Army into a pocket in the Spree Forest south of the Seelow Heights.

Volkssturm troops during what appears to be training exercise with a light MG 42 machine gun. These inexperienced men were given scant training before being sent to the front lines.

Phase 4: Spremberg–Torgau Offensive Operation, April 16–25

The Spremberg–Torgau offensive operation was the fourth sub-operation for the Berlin strategic offensive operation. Plans for the operation were put together on April 3 following a directive from Stavka which outlined that, along with the other three combined sub-operations, Konev's 1st Ukrainian Front was to prepare it forces against German positions that were digging in around the Cottbus area and to the region south of the Reich capital. Soviet forces were to capture the line between Beelitz and Wittenberg and advance along the Elbe River in the direction of the razed city of Dresden. Simultaneously, the 1st Ukrainian Front was ordered to prepare for the capture of Berlin and advance on Leipzig and deliver a blow against German units regrouping between Spremberg and Belzig.

However, Konev wanted the prize of being the first army front to capture Berlin. For this reason, if Stalin gave him freedom of movement into the city, at a moment's notice he planned to divert his right wing comprising two Guards tank armies operating to the northwest of Berlin. His left wing was to lead the Cottbus–Potsdam offensive operation northwest of Berlin and concurrently drive enemy formations west toward Spremberg. In front of him was the 4th Panzer Army, which was strung out around Spremberg and which was defending the river lines of the Neisse and Spree. This army comprised LVIII Panzer Corps, Panzer Corps Grossdeutchland, V Corps, and Corps Group Moser.

Armor of Konev's 1st Ukrainian Front in the Spremberg area, April 16. An ISU-152 fords a river onto the western bank.

An ISU-122 crosses a pontoon bridge, possibly across the River Spree.

An SU-100 tank destroyer fords the Spree. Introduced in the Red Army in October 1944, the SU-100 quickly became very popular. It saw extensive service during operations in and outside Berlin.

A young grenadier in a trench with various weapons at his disposal, including a Panzerfaust, Stg 44 assault rifle, and a Mauser self-loading Gewehr 41 rifle.

Artillerymen arm a BM-13 Katyusha rocket launcher on the edge of a town.

A battery of BM-13-16 launchers in action against an enemy target. A typical battery included four firing trucks and two technical support vehicles, with a crew of six for each truck.

A graphic image of a German soldier in a trench. The stress etched on his face is clear.

An exhausted MG 42 machine gunner rests on the side of a road.

A German Pak crew in action against advancing Soviet armor.

On April 16, Konev launched his operation with a massive artillery barrage followed by an armored attack supported by massed infantry which immediately secured parts of the Spree River north of Spremberg. Two Soviet armies in the south then seized bridgeheads in the region, driving back the overwhelmed German forces between Spremberg and Cottbus. What followed saw the Soviet 13th Army thrust deeply into the collapsing German lines, covering almost 14 miles in one day. The Germans attempted to consolidate around Spremberg to stem the Red Army's westward advance.

On April 19, mechanized units of the 4th Guards Tank Army and the 5th Guards Army bulldozed their way west, smashing through German defensive positions and bypassing Spremberg. Those German forces that did manage to break out clawed their way back onto the eastern bank of the Spree River, threatening Soviet units that were advancing west. Fearing that Spremberg would be turned into one of Hitler's fortresses, Konev immediately ordered the town be stormed. Through April 20 Soviet forces began flanking maneuvers around Spremberg. Later that day it was surrounded on three sides by massed artillery of the 3rd and 17th Artillery Divisions.

At nightfall the assault on Spremberg began with a massive artillery bombardment, followed by an infantry assault by the 33rd Guards Corps. Within two hours the town fell, allowing forward units of the 5ths Guards Army to advance west. Remnants of the German forces that had escaped what became known as the Spremberg encirclement broke out northwest through the forest to join General Walther Wenck's 12th Army. Many German units escaped to the town of Krausche, which was already in Soviet hands. Red Army units holding Krausche were overwhelmed by Germans troops as they flooded in from Spremberg.

While operations were continuing around Krausche, on the extreme left of Konev's offensive the Polish 2nd Army was involved in heavy fighting around the town of Bautzen, where between 21 and April 30 some 90,000 Polish troops—supported by

An SU-100 on the advance. By April 23, the 5th Guards Army had eliminated most of the German defenses around Spremberg.

Soviet soldiers and female personnel pose next to a knocked-out T-34-85 on a highway. On the bridge behind them are two abandoned Jagdpanzer 38 Hetzers.

20,000 troops of the Soviet 52nd Army and the 5th Guards Army—fought remnants of the 4th Panzer Army and the 17th Army. Across open fields and woods including German hamlets, Polish, Soviet, and German forces fought several brutal actions, including heavy urbanized fighting inside Bautzen itself. Several German units were well dug in and, armed with an assorted collection of Panzerfausts supported by heavy machine guns, pitched a series of well-fought battles. As a result of the German resistance the Polish 2nd Army suffered heavy losses, but supported by Soviet reserves it managed to prevent the Germans breaking through to the rear.

The main German objective in the area was to stop the 1st Ukrainian Front from breaking out through to Berlin and prevent Busse's 9th Army of 80,000 troops from being annihilated. The 4th Panzer Army—comprising some 50,000 soldiers of mixed quality, Luftwaffe and Hitlerjugend personnel, 300 tanks and self-propelled guns, and a mix of artillery and flak gun—was given the task of relieving the 9th Army.

The famous photograph taken on April 26 showing the American and Soviet linkup at the Elbe River between the 69th U.S. Infantry Division and 58th Soviet Guards Rifle Division. The following day in the Wittenberg area, the 1st Ukrainian Front captured bridgeheads on the western bank of the Elbe.

A staged photograph of American and Soviet soldiers during the historic linkup at Torgau.

Meanwhile, fighting around Bautzen was still raging, with determined German troops trying to recapture the town. Over the course of several days, pockets of German resistance strengthened, and bloody urbanized fighting ensued. On April 24 Bautzen was retaken by the Germans in one of the last victories by the Wehrmacht on what was left of the Eastern Front. However, despite the German victory, the battle had no strategic impact on the defense of Berlin. Yet, the town and surrounding area were held grimly by German forces until the end of the war, with the Germans suffering significant casualties.

Elsewhere in the region, the 1st Ukrainian Front continued to push west to the River Elbe against intermittent German resistance. On April 25, 5th Guards Army troops met American soldiers from the 69th Division of the U.S. First Army south of Torgau on the Elbe. This finally sealed the fate of Berlin from the south and ended the Spremberg–Torgau offensive. The Americans were ordered to halt at the Elbe to allow the Soviets to take Berlin.

In Profile:
General Ferdinand Schörner
June 12, 1892–July 2, 1973

Schörner, commander of Army Group Center, was one of the harshest and most-feared generals on the Eastern Front. In fact, in January 1945 he issued the order that all troops not fighting along the front without clear orders were to be hanged. He was totally unsympathetic to any units that withdrew from their lines and was brutal with his field commanders who gave up positions and lost ground. He

sent out an instruction that any officers who withdrew without his explicit orders were to be court-martialed on the spot for desertion. True to his word, during operations through 1945 many soldiers were hanged. As a result of these extreme measures, officers and soldiers alike came to despise him. Schörner, however, was a fanatical Hitler devotee and wholeheartedly supported his ideological and political ideas, becoming respected among high-level Nazis like Joseph Goebbels. On April 5, 1945, Schörner was promoted to field marshal and was named as the new commander in chief of the German Army High Command or OKH, Oberkommando des Heeres. Schörner's barbaric measures against his men and his later promotion changed nothing on the battlefield.

(Bundesarchiv Bild 183-L29176)

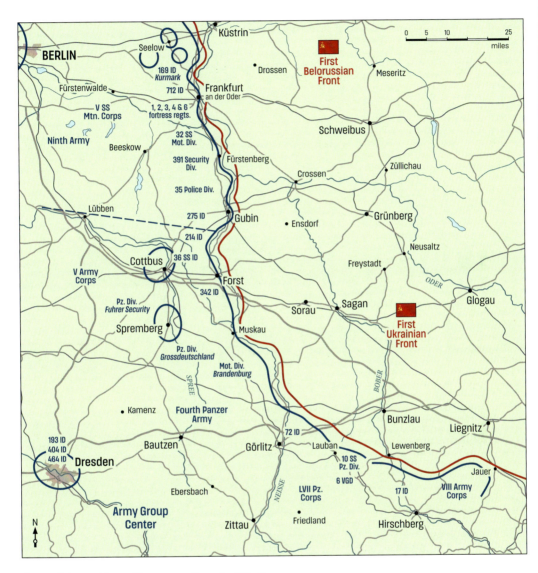

General disposition of forces southeast of Berlin.

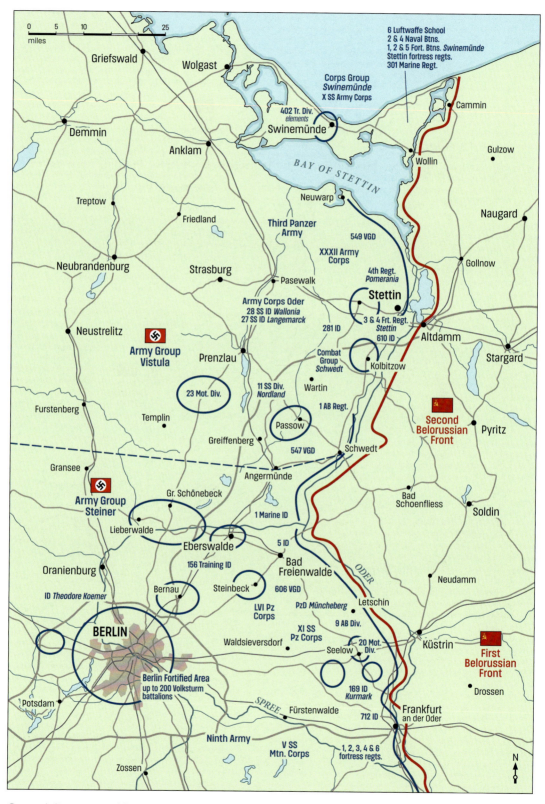

General disposition of forces northeast of Berlin.

Phase 5: Encirclement of the Reich Capital

Following three days of heavy fighting for the Seelow Heights that saw the loss of some seven hundred Red Army tanks and thousands of soldiers killed or wounded, the German 9th and 4th Panzer Armies were forced to undertake a fighting retreat. The German withdrawal meant that Zhukov's 1st Belorussian Front could now move forward in a wide pincer movement with Konev's 1st Ukrainian Front to trap the German forces. With the Western Allies now halted on the River Elbe, Soviets were left to capture Berlin themselves. In front of Zhukov, nothing but decimated German lines lay between him and the city. By the end of April 19, the German front north of Frankfurt to Seelow and to the area south ceased to exist. This allowed the breakthrough of the two Soviet fronts to envelop the German 9th Army east of Frankfurt in what became known as the battle of the Halbe Pocket. With German forces outside Berlin being slowly and systematically pulverized into submission by overwhelming firepower, the 1st Belorussian Front was finally able to move to the eastern and northeastern parts of the outer limits of the city.

On April 20, Hitler's birthday was celebrated with a massive artillery barrage by the 79th Rifle Corps of the 1st Belorussian Front. This allowed for the main strike force to press against Berlin, striking southwest past Müncheberg to Fürstenwalde behind the 9th Army. To the northeast of the capital, the 1st Ukrainian Front drove through a string of German defensive positions against the northern wing between Stettin and Schwedt, while the 2nd Belorussian Front made several heavy attacks against the northern flank of Army Group Vistula held by remnants of the 3rd Panzer Army.

A 1st Guards Tank Army ISU 152 crossing a pontoon bridge, April 1945.

Colonel Abram Temnik, commander of the 1st Guards Tank Brigade, 1st Guards Tank Army, seated in the front of an American Jeep.

The next day, April 21, the 2nd Guards Tank Army reported it had advanced almost thirty miles north of Berlin, with an attack carried out by advanced units southwest of Werneuchen. Although progress by the Soviets was relatively good despite stiff resistance, the Soviet command wanted to first complete the encirclement of the city and then envelop the German 9th Army. This army was already encircled at Forst and what was left of its corps were fanatically clinging to positions along what was known as the Berlin–Cottbus Highway line. Army Group Center had meanwhile committed its forces in a counteroffensive aimed at trying to break into Berlin around Bautzen. In the heavy fighting that ensued in front of Berlin, Heinrici appealed to Hitler, outlining that unless the 9th Army was withdrawn from their defensive positions they would be overrun and consequently destroyed, leaving the capital wide open for a ground attack. Heinrici made it clear to the Führer that the army could no longer move northwest of the city and would have no choice other than to withdraw westward.

Elsewhere, the 2nd Belorussian Front made several successful attacks against the 3rd Panzer Army and secured a bridgehead almost 10 miles deep on the west bank of the Oder. German troops comprising

A Soviet armored column on the move south of Berlin.

A column of T-34 tanks draped with infantry and halted outside Berlin.

Luftwaffe and Kriegsmarine personnel, Hitlerjugend, Volkssturm, Heer, and Waffen-SS personnel were now anxiously erecting defensive positions in the suburbs of Berlin as reports filtered through of a Soviet tank spearhead penetrating parts of the inner defensive ring of the city.

By April 22, Berlin was within range of field artillery. Red Army artillery units and Katyusha rocket-launcher batteries began preparing their weapons for a massive ground bombardment on the city. Up to now, Berliners had been exposed to constant long-range air and mortar attacks, spending many hours hidden in basements and cellars. Although they had been subjected to merciless bombardments, they believed or hoped that the Soviets were being held outside the city.

An ISU-152 in the suburbs of Berlin. This was a potent self-propelled vehicle and was regarded as a crucial weapon in urban combat operations.

An ISU-122 of the 3rd Guards Tank Army in a town south of Berlin. Following the encirclement of the capital, the army advanced north into the suburbs of the city.

On April 23, while Soviet plans were being finalized to enter Berlin, the 1st Belorussian Front and 1st Ukrainian Front continued compressing German forces to complete the encirclement of the city before the battle inside the capital began. For the next 24 hours, the Red Army worked methodically to complete its great ring around the city. From the north and east, Red Army formations fought their way through toward the S-Bahn defense ring. Using a method of wide-sweeping penetrating maneuvers, tanks supported by massed infantry of the 1st Belorussian and 1st Ukrainian Fronts linked up at Bohnsdorf, cutting

The 2nd Belorussian Front made several heavy attacks against the northern flank of Army Group Vistula, which was held by remnants of the 3rd Panzer Army. Thousands of troops were encircled and those who survived surrendered. Here a column of German POWs trudge past a T-34 tank.

T-34 tanks operating in one of many towns and villages almost razed to the ground by heavy fighting outside Berlin.

the last link between the German 9th Army and the capital. The encirclement of Berlin was sealed, which included the total isolation of the 9th Army still resisting in the Halbe region. The 4th Guards Tank Army reported it had reached the lakes at Potsdam, and the 2nd Guards Tank Army, advancing at speed from the north, reached Neuen and Spandau.

Elsewhere, disaster began to play out as the 2nd Belorussian Front smashed through the last reserves of the 3rd Panzer Army which was defending around Prenzlau. With the great jaws of the Red Army now fully closed around Berlin, German troops fighting outside the city could no longer influence the events that were about to unfold in the burning capital. Yet despite the dire situation in which the German command found themselves, there were plans for a relief operation using General Wenck's 12th Army. However, it was soon realized that with the city fully encircled, the operation would merely act as a wedge to temporarily wrench open the encirclement which would allow Berlin civilians to escape. Another relief operation was proposed with Felix Steiner's III SS Panzer Corps which would involve opening a corridor between the Red Army and American forces, and then advancing in the direction of Belzig. The 9th Army was ordered to break out and drive the remnants of its forces west to the Baruth–Zossen road. The 12th Army was then to linkup with the 9th Army and relieve Berlin.

Hitlerjugend soldiers defending a rubble-strewn street in the suburbs of Berlin, April 1945.

In Profile:
Heer Grenadiers with Sturmgewehr 44 and Panzerfaust

Grenadier with Sturmgewehr 44, 1097th Grenadier Regiment, XXXII Corps, 3rd Panzer Army, Defense of the Oder, April 1945. (Renato Dalmaso)

A German grenadier wearing the familiar M43 field cap and reversible parka with matching pants which are tucked into his high black leather marching boots. He is armed with the StG 44 (Sturmgewehr 44, "assault rifle 44"). Unusually, he is not wearing a black leather belt with ammunition pouches. In his left hand he holds a rolled-up *zeltbahn* (waterproof cape).

Panzerfaust Grenadier, 610th Infantry Division, 3rd Panzer Army, Oder Corps, Defense of the Oder, April 1945. (Renato Dalmaso)

A German grenadier wears an M40 steel helmet and reversible parka with matching pants which are secured to his short black leather marching boots by puttees. He wears the standard infantryman's black leather belt with rifle ammunition pouches for his Karabiner 98k bolt-action rifle slung over his back. Tucked into his belt is a Stg24 stick grenade. On his right shoulder is the Panzerfaust.

Soviet armor together with a column of support vehicles on the edge of the Halbe Forest.

A Russian photograph showing the devastation in the wake of the battle of Halbe—a convoy of German vehicles destroyed in the Halbe Forest.

Waffen-SS and Heer troops cross a damaged bridge over the River Elbe. They are survivors of what became known by the Germans as the "Slaughter at Halbe."

Soviet Order of Battle, April 16, 1945

NORTH BERLIN

2ND BELORUSSIAN FRONT (Rokossovsky)

2nd Shock Army (Fedyuninsky)

98th Rifle Corps
142nd Rifle Division
281st Rifle Division
381st Rifle Division

108th Rifle Corps
46th Rifle Division
90th Rifle Division
372nd Rifle Division

116th Rifle Corps
86th Rifle Division
321st Rifle Division
326th Rifle Division
161st Fortified Region

8th Guards Tank Corps

58th Guards Tank Brigade

59th Guards Tank Brigade

60th Guards Tank Brigade

28th Guards Motorized Rifle Brigade

65th Army (Batov)

18th Rifle Corps

15th Rifle Division

37th Guards Rifle Division

69th Rifle Division

46th Rifle Corps

108th Rifle Division

186th Rifle Division

413th Rifle Division

105th Rifle Corps

44th Guards Rifle Division

193rd Rifle Division

354th Rifle Division

70th Army (Popov)

47th Rifle Corps

71st Rifle Division

136th Rifle Division

162nd Rifle Division

96th Rifle Corps

1st Rifle Division

38th Guards Rifle Division

165th Rifle Division

114th Rifle Corps

76th Guards Rifle Division

160th Rifle Division

300th Rifle Division

49th Army (Grishin)

70th Rifle Corps

139th Rifle Division

238th Rifle Division

121st Rifle Corps

42nd Rifle Division

199th Rifle Division

380th Rifle Division

19th Army (Romanovsky)

40th Guards Rifle Corps

10th Guards Rifle Division

101st Guards Rifle Division

102nd Guards Rifle Division

132nd Rifle Corps

18th Rifle Division

27th Rifle Division

313th Rifle Division

134th Rifle Corps

205th Rifle Division

272nd Rifle Division

310th Rifle Division

3rd Artillery Corps

1st Artillery Division

18th Machine Gun Artillery Division

5th Guards Tank Army (Volsky)

29th Tank Corps
53rd Motorized Rifle Brigade
25th Tank Brigade
31st Tank Brigade
32nd Tank Brigade

Front Reserve

3rd Guards Cavalry Corps
5th Guards Cavalry Division
6th Guards Cavalry Division
32nd Cavalry Division
26th Artillery Division

1st Guards Tank Corps
1st Guards Motorized Rifle Brigade
15th Guards Tank Brigade
16th Guards Tank Brigade
17th Guards Tank Brigade

3rd Guards Tank Corps
2nd Guards Motorized Rifle Brigade
3rd Guards Tank Brigade
18th Guards Tank Brigade
19th Guards Tank Brigade

8th Motorized Corps
66th Motorized Rifle Brigade
67th Motorized Rifle Brigade
68th Motorized Rifle Brigade
116th Tank Brigade

CENTRAL BERLIN
1ST BELORUSSIAN FRONT (Zhukov)

61st Army (Belov)

9th Guards Rifle Corps
12th Guards Rifle Division
76th Guards Rifle Division
77th Guards Rifle Division
97th Rifle Division
110th Rifle Division
336th Rifle Division
356th Rifle Division
415th Rifle Division
12th Anti-Tank Artillery Brigade
68th Tank Brigade
36th Tank Regiment
1539th Self-Propelled Artillery Regiment
31st Railroad Armored Regiment
45th Railroad Armored Regiment
310th Engineer Battalion
344th Engineer Battalion
60th Guards Artillery Regiment
67th Guards Artillery Regiment
554th Artillery Regiment
547th Mortar Artillery Regiment
533rd Anti-Tank Artillery Regiment
1282nd Anti-Aircraft Artillery Regiment
13th Anti-Aircraft Artillery Division

1065th Anti-Aircraft Artillery Regiment

1173rd Anti-Aircraft Artillery Regiment

1175th Anti-Aircraft Artillery Regiment

1218th Anti-Aircraft Artillery Regiment

1st Polish Army (no details of commander)

1st Infantry Division

2nd Infantry Division

3rd Infantry Division

4th Infantry Division

6th Infantry Division

1st Armored Brigade

1st Cavalry Brigade

1st Gun Artillery Brigade

2nd Howitzer Artillery Brigade

3rd Army Artillery Brigade

5th Heavy Artillery Brigade

13th Self-Propelled Artillery Regiment

1st Anti-Aircraft Artillery Division

4th Anti-Tank Artillery Brigade

1st Sapper Brigade

2nd Sapper Brigade

1st Mortar Brigade (Reserve)

47th Army (Perkhorovich)

77th Rifle Corps

185th Rifle Division

234th Rifle Division

328th Rifle Division

125th Rifle Corps

60th Rifle Division

76th Rifle Division

175th Rifle Division

129th Rifle Corps

146th Rifle Division

82nd Rifle Division

132nd Rifle Division

70th Independent Guard Heavy Tank Regiment

334th Guards Heavy Self-Propelled Artillery Regiment

1204th Self-Propelled Artillery Regiment

1416th Self-Propelled Artillery Regiment

1892nd Self-Propelled Artillery Regiment

6th Breakthrough Artillery Division

2nd Mortar Brigade

10th Cannon Artillery Brigade

18th Howitzer Artillery Brigade

21st Light Artillery Brigade

118th Heavy Howitzer Artillery Brigade

124th Howitzer Artillery Brigade

4th Corps Artillery Brigade

74th Anti-Aircraft Artillery Division

18th Engineer Brigade

132nd Rifle Corps

143rd Rifle Division

260th Rifle Division

30th Guards Gun-Artillery Brigade

31st Anti-Aircraft Artillery Division

1488th Anti-Tank Artillery Regiment

163rd Anti-Tank Artillery Regiment

460th Mortar Regiment

75th Rocket Launcher Regiment

70th Guards Independent Tank Regiment

3rd Shock Army (Kuznetsov)

7th Rifle Corps
146th Rifle Division
265th Rifle Division
364th Rifle Division

9th Tank Corps
23rd Tank Brigade
95th Tank Brigade
108th Tank Brigade
8th Motor Rifle Brigade

12th Guards Rifle Corps
23rd Guards Rifle Division
33rd Guards Rifle Division
52nd Guards Rifle Division

79th Rifle Corps
150th Rifle Division
171st Rifle Division
207th Rifle Division

Engineers
25th Sapper Brigade

5th Pontoon Bridging Brigade

13th Pontoon Bridging Brigade

Artillery etc.
136th Gun-Artillery Brigade

1203rd Separate Self-Propelled Assault Artillery Regiment

1728th Separate Self-Propelled Assault Artillery Regiment

1729th Separate Self-Propelled Assault Artillery Regiment

45th Anti-Tank Brigade

5th Shock Army (Berzarin)

26th Guards Rifle Corps
89th Guards Rifle Division
95th Guards Rifle Division
266th Guards Rifle Division

9th Rifle Corps
230th Rifle Division
248th Rifle Division
301st Rifle Division

32nd Rifle Corps
60th Guards Rifle Division
295th Rifle Division
416th Rifle Division

6th Artillery & 20th Penetration Corps
2nd Artillery Penetration Division

20th Light Artillery Brigade

16th Guards Gun Artillery Brigade

4th Guards Heavy Howitzer Artillery Brigade

121st High-Power Howitzer Artillery Brigade

5th Mortar Brigade

68th Artillery Reconnaissance Battalion

14th Artillery Penetration Division

169th Light Artillery Brigade

172nd Howitzer Artillery Brigade

176th Heavy Howitzer Artillery Brigade

122nd High-Power Howitzer Artillery Brigade

21st Heavy Mortar Brigade

24th Mortar Brigade

6th Guards Mortar Brigade

112th Artillery Reconnaissance Battalion

44th Guards Cannon Artillery Brigade

124th Howitzer Artillery Brigade

32nd Special-Power Artillery Battalion

322nd Special-Power Artillery Battalion

331st Special-Power Artillery Battalion

3rd Guards Anti-Tank Artillery Brigade

4th Guards Anti-Tank Artillery Brigade

39th Anti-Tank Artillery Brigade

507th Tank-Destroyer Regiment

35th Guards Mortar Brigade

489th Mortar Regiment

2nd Guards Mortar Brigade

25th Guards Mortar Brigade

37th Guards Mortar Regiment

92nd Guards Mortar Regiment

2nd Guards Anti-Aircraft Artillery Division

302nd Guards Anti-Aircraft Artillery Regiment

303rd Guards Anti-Aircraft Artillery Regiment

304th Guards Anti-Aircraft Artillery Regiment

306th Guards Anti-Aircraft Artillery Regiment

1617th Anti-Aircraft Artillery Regiment

4th Separate Artillery Observation Balloon Battalion

22nd Artillery Penetration Division

6th Heavy Mortar Brigade

32nd Mortar Brigade

41st Guards Mortar Brigade

97th Heavy Howitzer Artillery Brigade

11th Tank Corps

20th Tank Brigade

36th Tank Brigade

65th Tank Brigade

12th Motorized Rifle Brigade

50th Guards Heavy Tank Regiment

1071st Light Artillery Regiment

1461st SU Regiment

1493rd SU Regiment

93rd Motorcycle Battalion

243rd Mortar Regiment

115th Guards Mortar Battalion

1388th Anti-Aircraft Artillery Regiment

220th Tank Brigade

11th Guards Heavy Tank Brigade

67th Guards Heavy Tank Brigade

92nd Engineer Tank Regiment

396th Guards Heavy SU Regiment

1504th SU Regiment

61st Engineer-Sapper Brigade

8th Flamethrower Battalion

8th Guards Army (Chuikov)

4th Guards Rifle Corps

35th Guards Rifle Division

47th Guards Rifle Division

57th Guards Rifle Division

35th Guards Rifle Corps

(No details of subunits)

47th Guards Rifle Corps

28th Guards Rifle Corps

39th Guards Rifle Division

57th Guards Rifle Division

79th Guards Rifle Division

88th Guards Rifle Division

29th Guards Rifle Corps

27th Guards Rifle Division

74th Guards Rifle Division

82nd Guards Rifle Division

11th Tank Corps

20th Tank Brigade

36th Tank Brigade

65th Tank Brigade

12th Motorized Rifle Brigade

11th Independent Guards Heavy Tank Brigade

67th Guards Heavy Tank Brigade

220th Independent Tank Brigade

396th Guards Heavy Self-Propelled Artillery Regiment

1504th Independent Self-Propelled Artillery Regiment

6th Breakthrough Artillery Corps

2nd Breakthrough Artillery Division

5th Mortar Brigade

10th Guards Howitzer Artillery Brigade

16th Guards Canon Artillery Brigade

20th Light Artillery Brigade

48th Guards Heavy Howitzer Artillery Brigade

121st Howitzer Artillery Brigade

14th Breakthrough Artillery Division

6th Guards Mortar Brigade

21st Heavy Mortar Brigade

24th Mortar Brigade

122nd Howitzer Artillery Brigade

169th Light Artillery Brigade

172nd Howitzer Artillery Brigade

176th Heavy Howitzer Artillery Brigade

22nd Breakthrough Artillery Division

6th Heavy Mortar Brigade

32nd Mortar Brigade

97th Heavy Howitzer Brigade

2nd Guards Mortar Brigade

25th Guards Mortar Brigade

35th Guards Mortar Brigade

2nd Guards Anti-Aircraft Artillery Division

1st Independent Guards Motorized Engineer Brigade

17th Breakthrough Engineer Brigade

61st Engineer Brigade

69th Army (Kolpakchi)

161st Rifle Division

180th Rifle Division

270th Rifle Division

1st Destroyer Division

37th Rifle Brigade

173rd Tank Brigades

33rd Army (Tsvetayev)

16th Rifle Corps

323rd Rifle Division

339th Rifle Division

383rd Rifle Division

62nd Rifle Corps

95th Rifle Division

222nd Rifle Division

362nd Rifle Division

49th Rifle Division

115th Fortified Region

119th Fortified Region

16th Air Army (Rudenko)

3rd Bomber Aviation Corps (Finow, Eastern Germany)

183rd Bomber Aviation Division (Oranienburg, Eastern Germany)

241st Bomber Aviation Division (Werneuchen, Eastern Germany)

301st Bomber Aviation Division (Finow, Eastern Germany)

6th Bomber Aviation Corps (Szprotava, Poland)

113th Bomber Aviation Division (Poznan-Kreising, Poland)

326th Bomber Aviation Division (Sagan, Poland)

334th Bomber Aviation Division (Poznan-Lawica, Poland)

6th Assault Aviation Corps (Finsterwalde, Eastern Germany)

197th Assault Aviation Division (Strausberg, Eastern Germany)

198th Assault Aviation Division (Eastern Germany)

2nd Assault Aviation Division (Wittstock/Rechlin, Eastern Germany)

9th Assault Aviation Corps (Finsterwalde, Eastern Germany)

3rd Guards Assault Aviation Division (Finsterwalde, Eastern Germany)

300th Assault Aviation Division (Cottbus, Eastern Germany)

11th Guards Assault Aviation Division (Jüterbog-Altes Lager, Eastern Germany)

1st Guards Fighter Aviation Corps (Perleberg, Eastern Germany)

3rd Guards Fighter Aviation Division (Ludwigslust, Eastern Germany)

4th Guards Fighter Division (Perleberg, Eastern Germany)

240th Fighter Aviation Division (Tutow, Eastern Germany)

3rd Fighter Aviation Corps (Lager Döberitz-Falkensee, Eastern Germany)

265th Fighter Aviation Division (Brandenburg, Eastern Germany)

278th Fighter Aviation Division (Elstal, Eastern Germany)

286th Fighter Aviation Division (Dallgow, Eastern Germany)

13th Fighter Aviation Corps (Halle/Leipzig area, Germany)

193rd Fighter Aviation Division (Altenburg, Eastern Germany)

283rd Fighter Aviation Division (Köthen or Halle, Eastern Germany)

282nd Fighter Aviation Division (Grossenhain, Eastern Germany)

9th Guards Night-Bomber Aviation Division (Straussberg, Eastern Germany)

16th Independent Reconnaissance Aviation Regiment (Schönwalde, Eastern Germany)

93rd Independent Artillery Correction Regiment (Fürstenwalde, Eastern Germany)

98th Independent Artillery Correction Regiment (Zerbst, Eastern Germany)

226th Separate Mixed Wing (Sperenberg Airfield, Eastern Germany)

62nd Guards Aviation Regiment GVF (Berlin-Adlershof, Eastern Germany)

919th Independent Communications Aviation Squadron (Eastern Germany)

18th Air Army (Gastilovich)

1st Guards Smolensk Long-Range Bomber Air Corps

2nd Guards Bryansk Long-Range Bomber Aviation Corps

3rd Guards Stalingrad Long-Range Bomber Aviation Corps

4th Guards Gomel Long-Range Bomber Aviation Corps

6th Long-Range Aviation Corps

62nd Air Division Long Range

1st Guards Tank Army (Katukov)

8th Guards Mechanized Corps

19th Guards Mechanized Brigade

20th Guards Mechanized Brigade

21st Guard Mechanized Brigade

1st Guards Tank Brigade

48th Guards Separate Tank Regiment

353rd Guards Self-Propelled Artillery Regiment

400th Guards Self-Propelled Artillery Regiment

265th Guards Mortar Regiment

405th Guards Mortar Battalion

358th Guards Anti-Aircraft Artillery Regiment

8th Guards Motorcycle Battalion

11th Guards Tanks Corps

40th Guards Tank Brigade

44th Guards Tank Brigade

45th Guards Tank Brigade

27th Guards Motor Rifle Brigade

399th Guards Heavy Self-Propelled Artillery Regiment

362nd Guards Self-Propelled Artillery Regiment

1454th Self-Propelled Artillery Regiment

350th Light Artillery Regiment

270th Guards Mortar Regiment

53rd Guards Mortar Battalion

1018th Anti-Aircraft Artillery Regiment

9th Guards Motorcycle Battalion

Army Troops

64th Guards Tank Brigade

11th Guards Separate Tank Regiment

19th Light Self-Propelled Artillery Brigade

197th Light Artillery Brigade

79th Guards Mortar Regiment

17th Motorized Engineer Brigade

191st Guards Liaison Aviation Regiment

6th Motorcycle Regiment

12th Guards Motorcycle Regiment

2nd Guards Tank Army (Bogdanov)

3rd Tank Corps

50th Tank Brigade

51st Tank Brigade

103rd Tank Brigade

57th Motor Rifle Brigade

74th Motorcycle Battalion

881st Tank-Destroyer Regiment

728th Tank-Destroyer Battalion

234th Mortar Regiment

121st Anti-Aircraft Artillery Regiment

16th Tank Corps

107th Tank Brigade

109th Tank Brigade

164th Tank Brigade

15th Motor Rifle Brigade

51st Motorcycle Battalion

1441st Self-Propelled Artillery Regiment

614th Tank-Destroyer Regiment

729th Tank-Destroyer Battalion

226th Mortar Regiment

11th Guards Tank Brigade

87th Motorcycle Battalion

357th Engineer Battalion

3rd Army (Gorbatov)

35th Rifle Corps

250th Rifle Division

290th Rifle Division

348th Rifle Division

40th Rifle Corps

5th Rifle Division

129th Rifle Division

169th Rifle Divisions

41st Rifle Corps

120th Guards Division

269th Guards Division

283rd Rifle Divisions

Artillery

4th Corps Artillery Brigade

44th Gun Artillery Brigade

584th Anti-Tank Artillery Regiment

4th Artillery Corps

5th Breakthrough Artillery Division

12th Breakthrough Artillery Division

5th Guards Mortar Division

1002nd Communications Battalion

821st Separate Reconnaissance Artillery Battalion

2355th Military Postal Station

SOUTHWEST BERLIN
1ST UKRAINIAN FRONT
(Konev)

5th Guards Army (Zhadov)

32nd Guards Rifle Corps (Kolomiets)

(No details of subunits)

33rd Guards Rifle Corps

(No details of subunits)

34th Guards Rifle Corps

(No details of subunits)

3rd Penetration Artillery Division

155th Cannon Artillery Brigade

10th Guards Fighter Anti-Tank Artillery Brigade

1073rd Fighter Anti-Tank Artillery Regiment

1075th Fighter Anti-Tank Artillery Regiment

469th Mortar Regiment

308th Guards Mortar Regiment

29th Anti-Aircraft Artillery Division

Engineers
3rd Pontoon Bridge Brigade
55th Engineer Sapper Brigade

4th Guards Tank Corps
150th Tank Brigade
39th Separate Tank Regiment
226th Separate Tank Regiment
1889th Self-Propelled Artillery Regiment

2nd Polish Army (Swierczewski)
5th Infantry Division
7th Infantry Division
8th Infantry Division
9th Infantry Division
10th Infantry Division
2nd Artillery Division
6th Light Artillery Brigade
7th Howitzer Artillery Brigade
8th Heavy Artillery Brigade
3rd Anti-Aircraft Artillery Division
9th Anti-Tank Brigade
14th Anti-Tank Brigade
3rd Mortar Regiment

1st Tank Corps
16th Tank Brigade
5th Heavy Tank Regiment
28th Armored Artillery Regiment
4th Sapper Brigade

52nd Army (Koroteev)

7th Guards Mechanized Corps
(No details of subunits)

48th Rifle Corps
116th Rifle Division
294th Rifle Division

73rd Rifle Corps
50th Rifle Division
111th Rifle Division
254th Rifle Division

78th Rifle Corps
31st Rifle Division
214th Rifle Division
373rd Rifle Division
213th Rifle Division
214th Tank Regiment

4th Guards Tank Army (Swierczewski)
11th Ural Volunteer Tank Corps
30th Ural Volunteer Tank Corps
6th Guard Mechanized Corps

28th Army (Koroteev)

3rd Guards Rifle Corps
50th Guards Rifle Division
54th Guards Rifle Division
96th Guards Rifle Divisions

20th Rifle Corps
(No details of subunits)

48th Rifle Corps

55th Guards Rifle Divisions

20th Rifle Division

128th Rifle Corps

(No details of subunits)

61st Rifle Corps

(No details of subunits)

130th Rifle Corps

152nd Rifle Division

(No details of any additional
subunits)

3rd Corps Artillery Brigade

157th Cannon Artillery Brigade

377th Cannon Artillery Regiment

530th Fighter Anti-Tank Artillery
Regiment

1st Mortar Brigade

133rd Guards Mortar Regiment

316th Guards Mortar Regiments

12th Anti-Aircraft Artillery Division

836th Anti-Aircraft Artillery Regiment

977th Anti-Aircraft Artillery Regiment

990th Anti-Aircraft Artillery Regiment

997th Anti-Aircraft Artillery
Regiments

607th Anti-Aircraft Artillery Regiment

31st Army (Lelyushenko)

36th Rifle Corps

173rd Rifle Division

176th Rifle Division

352nd Rifle Division

44th Rifle Corps

62nd Rifle Division

174th Rifle Division

220th Rifle Division

71st Rifle Corps

54th Rifle Division

88th Rifle Division

331st Rifle Division

140th Gun-Artillery Brigade

51st Guards Tank-Destroyer Regiment

357th Guards Tank-Destroyer
Regiment

529th Tank-Destroyer Regiment

549th Mortar Regiment

1478th Anti-aircraft Artillery
Regiment

926th SU Regiment

959th SU Regiment

31st Engineer-Sapper Brigade

3rd Guards Army
(Luchinsky)

14th Rifle Corps

50th Guards Rifle Division

197th Rifle Division

203rd Rifle Division

278th Rifle Division

90th Separate Rifle Brigade

94th Separate Rifle Brigade

1st Guards Mechanized Brigade

In Profile:
Soviet T-34-85 Tank and SU-76M Light Self-Propelled Gun

T-34-85 Tank, 5th Guards Tank Army, Stettin, April 19, 1945. (Oliver Missing)

This T-34-85 tank is painted in overall olive-green and displays white recognition marks horizontally across the turret and laterally on the cupola. Similar vehicles for the battle of Berlin were given these white painted stripes. Its tactical number "K239" is painted in white. To deflect hand grenades, the vehicle is fitted with what was known as bedspring armor.

SU-76M Soviet Light Self-Propelled Gun, 4th Guards Tank Army, Havel River, April 24, 1945. (Oliver Missing)

This SU-76M light self-propelled gun is painted in overall olive-green and displays white recognition marks horizontally across the crew compartment. There are no tactical markings on the vehicle. It was the second-most produced Soviet AFV of the war.

German Order of Battle, April 16, 1945

3rd Panzer Army (von Manteuffel)

Swinemünde Corps (Ansat)

2nd Marine Division

402nd Naval Division

522nd Grenadier Training Regiment Stab

27/172 Füsilier Training Battalion Rostock

94th Grenadier Training Battalion Rostock

4/222 Grenadier Training Battalion Rostock

48/374 Grenadier Training Battalion Neubrandenburg

89/368 Grenadier Training Battalion Schwerin

85th Hungarian Regiment Stab

Hungarian Infantry School Varpalota

Brigade Kopp

Alarm Regiment 4

Alarm Regiment 5

Stab Artillery Training Regiment 2 Schwerin

257th Artillery Ausbildung Battalion

12/32 Artillery Battalion

38/2 Artillery Battalion Schwerin

22nd Flak Training Battalion

XXXII Corps (Schack)

1st Panzerjäger Battalion

Kampfgruppe Voigt

Volkssturm Battalion 244

Volkssturm Battalion 26/50

Volkssturm Battalion 26/52

Volkssturm Battalion 26/62

281st Infantry Division

379th Regiment (part)

1098th Regiment (part)

Battalion Creuz

Volkssturm Battalion Hessen Nassau

1 Fortress Alarm Battalion

549th Volksgrenadier Division

1097th Grenadier Regiment (part)

1099th Grenadier Regiment (part)

1549th Artillery Regiment (part)

Other Units

1549th Pioneer Battalion

549th Replacement Battalion

549th Füsilier Battalion

549th Panzerjäger Battalion (part)

929th Heeres Artillery Battalion

3rd Flak Regiment

605th Heavy Flak Battalion (part)

325th Heavy Flak Battalion

474th Heavy Flak Battalion

437th Heavy Flak Battalion

Regiment Pommern 4 (part)

Marine Alarm Battalion

Recce Battalion, 4th SS Polizei Panzergrenadier Division

5th Jäger Division (part)

1 Hiterjugend Battalion

Volkssturm Battalion 26/11

Volkssturm Battalion 26/29

Volkssturm Battalion 26/70

SS-Latvian Feldersatz Depot

SS-Latvian Grenadier Regiment 1 (part)

SS-Latvian Grenadier Regiment 2 (part)

SS-Latvian Grenadier Regiment 3 (part)

Fortress Stettin

418th Grenadier Regiment (I. & II. Battalions) from 281st Security Division

281st Füsilier Battalion from 281st Security Division

1st Fortress Infantry Regiment (I. & II. Battalions), former 43rd Fortress Regiment (with 1453rd & 1454th Fortress Battalions)

2nd Fortress Infantry Regiment (I. & II. Battalions), former 44th Fortress Regiment (with 1455th & 1457th Fortress Battalions)

3rd Fortress Infantry Regiment (I. & II. Battalions), former Over & Roy Alarm Battalions

4th Fortress Infantry Regiment (I. & II. Battalions), former Benner & Laase Alarm Battalions

5th Fortress Infantry Regiment (I. & II. Battalions), former 1st Marine Infantry Battalion & Feldersatz Battalion + police company

85th Fortress MG Battalion

Stettin A Fortress MG Battalion

Fortress Pioneer Battalion

3132nd Artillery Regiment

3156th Fortress Flak Battalion

3158th Fortress Flak Battalion

VIII Fortress Pak Regiment

XVI Fortress Pak Verband

XXVII Fortress Pak Verband

725th Pioneer Battalion

555th z.v.B. Pioneer Regiment

Fire Security Battalion

96th Pioneer Battalion

254th Pioneer Battalion

IV Waffen-SS Grenadier Regiment

Oder Corps (von dem Bach-Zelewski)

Fs E. u. A. Regiment 1

284th Sturmgeschütze Brigade

Infantry Group Klossek

1604th (Soviet) Regiment (part)

89/IV Hungarian Battalion

Volkssturm Battalion Genssen

1 Battalion F. A. Oder

II./3 SS Regiment

610th Infantry Division

Volkssturm Battalion Hamburg

Volkssturm Battalion Brandenburg

Army Group Reserve

III SS Panzer Corps (Steiner)

27th SS Grenadier Division

Assigned to 3rd Panzer Army

66th SS Volunteer Grenadier Regiment (part)

67th SS Volunteer Grenadier Regiment (part)

27th SS Volunteer Artillery Regiment (part)

28th SS Grenadier Division

Assigned to 3rd Panzer Army

69th SS Volunteer Grenadier Regiment (part)

70th SS Volunteer Grenadier Regiment (part)

28th SS Volunteer Artillery Regiment (part)

28th SS Volunteer Pioneer Battalion

503rd SS Heavy Panzer Battalion

Assigned to 9th Army

11th SS Panzergrenadier Division

Assigned to 9th Army

11th SS Panzer Regiment Hermann von Salza (part)

23rd SS Grenadier Regiment (part)

24th SS Grenadier Regiment (part)

11th SS Artillery Regiment (part)

11th SS Panzer Recce Battalion (part)

11th SS Pioneer Battalion

23rd SS Panzergrenadier Division

Assigned to 9th Army

48th SS Volunteer Grenadier Regiment (part)

49th SS Volunteer Grenadier Regiment (part)

54th SS Volunteer Artillery Regiment (part)

Berlin Garrison

9 defensive sectors created A to H and Z "Zentrum"

Wacht Regiment Berlin

SS Wachbataillon Reichführer

Fortress Regiments etc.

57th Fortress Regiment in Sector Anton

58th Fortress Regiment

59th Fortress Regiment in Sector Caesar

60th Fortress Regiment (part) in Sector Dora

61st Fortress Regiment

62nd Fortress Regiment (outside Berlin with Kampgruppe Steiner)

63rd Fortress Regiment

64th Fortress Regiment

65th Fortress Regiment

Landeschutzen Battalion 320 in Sector A

213th Sicherungs Battalion

Festungs PAK Ausbildungs-und Ersatz Einheit 101

Festungs PAK Verband XXI

1st Flak Division

126th Flak Regiment (Nord)

202nd Heavy Flak Battalion

530th Heavy Flak Battalion

5./437 (5 × 10.5 cm) Dahlem Staats

7./437 (5 × 10.5 cm) Eichkamp

9./212 (6 ital.) Trabrennd Ruhleben

4./605 (6) Grunewald

4./126 (5 × 10.5 cm) Ruhleben

2./422 (8 ital.) Jungfernheide

3./211 (6) Blumeshof

3./126 (6 × 10.5 cm) Tegel: Schiesspl.

2./215 v (4 × 41) Dreipfuhl

3./215 v (3 × 10.5 cm) Sven-Hedin Strasse

123rd Heavy Flak Battalion (Turm)

1./123rd battery (4 × 12.8 cm) Friedrichshain

2./123rd battery (4 × 12.8 cm) Zoo

3. 123rd Battery (3 × 12.8 cm) Humbolthain

733rd Light Flak Battalion

z.b.V. 6524 Battery (6 × 3.7 cm + 3 × 2cm) Flh Brandenburg Briest

7./733 Battery (12 × 3.7 cm? + 3 × 2 cm) Flh Brandenburg Briest

1./755 Battery (3 × 3.7 cm + 12 × 2 cm) Sector H

22nd Flak Regiment (Süd)

422nd Heavy Flak Battalion

7./326 (ital.) in Hospital Schöneweide

9./326 in Zentralviehof

z.b.V. 10306 (RAD 4/174) in Laubenkolonie Weissensee

2./605 in Karlshorst, Pionierschule

5./326 in Trainierbahn Karlshorst

4./307 in Friedrichsfelde-Ost

6./126 (6 × 10.5 cm) in Hohenschönhausen II

7./126 (5 × 10.5 cm) in Friedrichsfelde I

10./126 (6 × 10.5 cm) in Biesdorf

126th Heavy Flak Battalion

4./422 in Oberspree

5./126 (6 × 10.5 cm) in Schöneberg

10./326 in Treptower Park II

8./211 (RAD 4./145) in Stellung Treptower Park II

z.b.V. 10359 in Sportplatz Baumschulenweg

3./458 in Tempelhofer Feld

2./326 (RAD 3./52) in Stellung Bosporusweg

5./211 in Johannifer Stift

7./605 in Gradestrasse

6./307 (RAD 7./95) in Sportplatz Grenzallee

979th Light Flak Battalion

z.b.V. 14040 Battery (3 × 3.7 cm 43 + 3 × 3.7 cm) Sector C

z.b.V. 6524 Battery (3 × 3.7 cm) Sector C

1./733 Battery (15 × 3.7 cm ZW) Schönefeld

Sector Caesar

In construction

z.B.V. 10234 in Hospital Oberschöneweide

z.b.V. 10224 in Spertplatz Herzberge

233/III in Biesdorf I

Sector Dora

5./126 in Schöneberg

5./211 in Sportplatz Lichterfelde

Volkssturm

3/2 Volkssturm Battalion

3/3 Volkssturm Battalion

3/9 Volkssturm Battalion in Sector C

3/11 Volkssturm Battalion in Sector C

3/19 Volkssturm Battalion in Sector C

3/21 Volkssturm Battalion

3/24 Volkssturm Battalion

3/30 Volkssturm Battalion

3/36 Volkssturm Battalion

3/101 Volkssturm Battalion in Sector F

3/105 Volkssturm Battalion in Sector F

3/107 Volkssturm Battalion

3/109 Volkssturm Battalion in Sector F

3/110 Volkssturm Battalion

3/111 Volkssturm Battalion in Sector E

3/112 Volkssturm Battalion in Sector E

3/113 Volkssturm Battalion in Sector F

3/115 Siemensdorf Volkssturm Battalion in Sector A

3/119 Volkssturm Battalion

3/121 Volkssturm Battalion in Sector A

3/155 Volkssturm Battalion

3/164 Volkssturm Battalion

3/181 Volkssturm Battalion in Sector F

3/185 Volkssturm Battalion

3/191 Volkssturm Battalion

3/201 Volkssturm Battalion in Sector E

3/203 Volkssturm Battalion in Sector E

3/205 Volkssturm Battalion in Sector E

3/208 Volkssturm Battalion

16/209 Volkssturm Battalion

209 Volkssturm Battalion in Sector E

3/215 Volkssturm Battalion in Sector E

3/216 Volkssturm Battalion

268 Volkssturm Battalion

3/277 Volkssturm Battalion

3/301 Volkssturm Battalion

3/303 Volkssturm Battalion in Sector D

3/305 Volkssturm Battalion

3/306 Volkssturm Battalion in Sector D

3/307 Volkssturm Battalion in Sector D

3/309 Volkssturm Battalion in Sector C

3/311 Volkssturm Battalion

3/312 Volkssturm Battalion

3/313 Volkssturm Battalion

3/314 Volkssturm Battalion

3/316 Volkssturm Battalion in Sector D

3/320 Hitlerjugend Volkssturm Battalion

3/355 Volkssturm Battalion

3/403 Volkssturm Battalion in Sector G

3/405 Volkssturm Battalion

3/407 Volkssturm Battalion in Sector G

3/421 Volkssturm Battalion in Sector G

3/424 Volkssturm Battalion

3/425 Volkssturm Battalion in Sector E

3/427 Volkssturm Battalion

3/511 Volkssturm Battalion in Sector C

3/513 Volkssturm Battalion

3/515 Volkssturm Battalion

3/517 Volkssturm Battalion in Sector C

3/521 Volkssturm Battalion in Sector C

3/550 Volkssturm Battalion

3/556 Volkssturm Battalion

3/569 Volkssturm Battalion in Sector G

3/603 Volkssturm Battalion in Sector G

3/607 Volkssturm Battalion in Sector F

3/609 Volkssturm Battalion in Sector F

3/611 Volkssturm Battalion in Sector G

3/615 Volkssturm Battalion

3/617 Volkssturm Battalion in Sector G

3/628 Volkssturm Battalion

3/691 Volkssturm Battalion in Sector A

3/707 Volkssturm Battalion

3/709 Volkssturm Battalion

3/713 Volkssturm Battalion in Sector H

3/715 Volkssturm Battalion in Treptow

3/725 Volkssturm Battalion

3/803 Volkssturm Battalion in Sector H

3/804 Volkssturm Battalion in Sector A

3/805 Volkssturm Battalion in Sector A

3/806 Volkssturm Battalion in Sector A

3/811 Volkssturm Battalion

3/812 Volkssturm Battalion in Sector A

3/813 Volkssturm Battalion Hummel in Sector A

3/815 Volkssturm Battalion in Sector A

3/817 Volkssturm Battalion in Sector A

3/869 Volkssturm Battalion in Sector H

3/885 Volkssturm Battalion in Sector A

mot 3/891 Volkssturm Battalion in Sector A

mot 3/892 Volkssturm Battalion in Sector A

mot 3/894 Volkssturm Battalion in Sector A

3/909 Volkssturm Battalion in Sector B

3/917 Volkssturm Battalion in Sector B

3/919 Volkssturm Battalion in Sector B

3/921 Volkssturm Battalion in Treptow

3/922 Volkssturm Battalion in Treptow

Volkssturm Company Reichkanzeil in Sector Z

10 "Nominal" Volkssturm Pionier Battalions with 2,009 men

Abschnitt A 3 companies: 364 men

Abschnitt B 1 company: 152 men

Anschnitt C 1 company: 160 men

Abschnitt D 1 company: 130 men

Abschnitt E 4 companies: 366 men

Abschnitt F 1 company: 143 men

Abschnitt G 3 companies: 256 men

Abschnitt H 1 company: 169 men

Abschnitt Z 1 company: 205 men

Reserve 1 company: 64 men

In Profile:
General Theodor Busse
December 15, 1897–October 21, 1986

On January 21, 1945, Busse was given command of the 9th Army, part of Army Group Vistula. As the Red Army approached the Oder, he was ordered to specifically defend positions east of Berlin. Arguably, Busse was one of the most important generals during the battle for Berlin. He was a very capable commander, but came across as overbearing and excessively optimistic, which was one of his main downfalls. In front of his officers, he openly told them he believed that if the 9th Army could hold the Oder line long enough, it would allow the Americans to capture Berlin and save most of the Reich from Soviet occupation. However, when it became apparent that idea was unachievable, he ordered his troops to steadfastly defend their positions and make a series of strategic withdrawals westward to link with General Walter Wenck's 12th Army. To accomplish his strategy he defied Hitler's orders, including the OKH's. As a result of Busse's obdurate personality, he would ultimately save 40,000 of his 200,000 soldiers from annihilation.

In Profile:

Heer Grenadier and Volksgrenadier Squad

Grenadier, 17th Infantry Division, 4th Panzer Army, Bautzen, April 23, 1945. (Renato Dalmaso)

This grenadier is wearing the M35 steel helmet and the standard issue infantryman's greatcoat. He is armed with two bolt-action rifles due to the lack of ammunition pouches. Attached to his leather straps is a gas cape. On his back is his army-issue *tornister* canvas and fur backpack.

Volksgrenadier Squad, 545th Volksgrenadier Division, 4th Panzer Army, Bautzen, April 24, 1945. (Renato Dalmaso)

A squad of Volksgrenadiers wearing the Wehrmacht splinter camouflage field blouses with standard-issue army pants and short-shaft leather boots. They are armed with a variety of weapons ranging from the MP 40, Karabiner 98k bolt-action rifle, and the Gewehr self-loading rifle.

| Battle for Berlin

While the Red Army was completing the encirclement of Berlin, inside the city German forces were preparing their defenses. In total there were some 45,000 troops comprising a mixed collection of Heer, Waffen-SS, and Luftwaffe troops, supported by Hitlerjugend, Volkssturm, militia groups, and the Berlin Police.

SS-Brigadeführer Wilhelm Mohnke had been appointed the "defender of Berlin" for the central government district which encompassed Hitler's Reich Chancellery and the Führerbunker. Some 2,000 troops were at his disposal, organized into eight designated sectors in the central area of the city. To the north he placed the 9th Fallschirmjäger Division, while in the northeast Panzer Division Müncheberg prepared its positions. To the west of the capital, he placed remnants of the 20th Infantry Division, while to the east was the 11th SS Panzergrenadier Division Nordland. In reserve were elements of the 18th Panzergrenadier Division, which set up defenses in the central area.

On April 23, the 5th Shock Army and the 1st Guards Tank Army made a series of assaults from the southeast and fought several close-quarter actions against what was left of LVI Panzer Corps. By the following day Red Army troops had reached the Berlin S-Bahn railway line north of the Teltow Canal. What followed was heavy urbanized fighting with Soviet troops utilizing their armor through the rubble-strewn streets.

Fighting inside the city was ferocious: the Soviets adopted the same method of urbanized warfare as they had many times by battering their way one block after the next, fighting street by street among the rubble-strewn burning buildings. The Germans were hard pressed to defend their positions, but each soldier was aware of the significance of holding every foot of ground.

On April 26, the 8th Guards Tank Army, which had seen significant resistance in the southern suburbs, managed to reach and attack the Tempelhof Airport defended by the Müncheberg Division. Supporting these attacks from east to west of the capital was the 5th

Soviet artillery crew prepare to open fire in the suburbs of Berlin.

A Red Army howitzer being towed by an artillery tractor through the Berlin suburbs. Late on April 21 the 1st Belorussian Front's 47th Army, supported by the 2nd Guards Tank Army's 9th Guards Tank Corps, reached the Schmetzdorf line, the northeastern outskirts of Schildow, while the 125th and 129th Rifle Corps reached the northeastern outskirts of Buchholz.

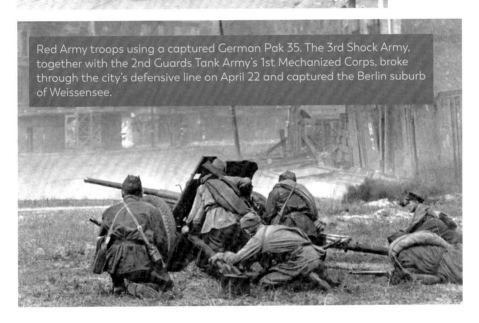

Red Army troops using a captured German Pak 35. The 3rd Shock Army, together with the 2nd Guards Tank Army's 1st Mechanized Corps, broke through the city's defensive line on April 22 and captured the Berlin suburb of Weissensee.

A Soviet Flak crew scan the skies for possible enemy aircraft, April 22. On this day the 5th Shock Army, supported by the 2nd Guards Tank Army's 12th Guards Tank Corps, broke through the city's defensive line and reached the western outskirts of Hohenschönhausen, Marzahn, Wuhlgarten, and Altlandsberg.

Red Army troops on a Berlin street prepare to open fire. Heavy artillery supported the 8th Guards Army and the 1st Guards Tank Army as they fought along the city's defensive line between Eggersdorf and Erkner.

Red Army officers in front of a burning building.

Red Army riflemen pause for a smoke break in the eastern part of the city. By April 25 the 5th Shock Army, supported by the 11th Tank Corps, was fighting here, clearing the Biesdorf, Friedrichsfelde, and Karlshorst suburbs.

A Red Army tank destroyer fights its way along a Berlin street.

IS-2 tanks in the city. By the end of the day on April 25 the 4th Guards Tank Army, supported by the 10th Guards Tank Corps, had reached the western outskirts of Zehlendorf, southern Caputh, Potsdam.

A T-34-85 of the 7th Guards Tank Army advances along a street supported by riflemen.

Shock Army, 1st Guards Tank Army, and the 3rd Guards Tank Army. Along the streets, inside houses and shops, German soldiers tried to defend their positions using Panzerfausts to knock out advancing Soviet tanks. Even when they found themselves almost completely cut off, there was still stubborn refusal to capitulate. As a consequence, Red Army troops spent hours clearing streets and buildings, often using flamethrowers to eliminate enemy resistance.

The Soviets advanced deeper into the city, continuing to batter their way through it. Often, they came across German positions that were no more than barricaded defenses comprising burned-out trams, vehicles, and other materials scraped together from the decimated streets.

By April 27 the Germans, notably remnants of the Müncheberg and Nordland Divisions, were being pushed farther back into the center district of the city with Soviet forces assaulting along the main axes from the southeast, along the Frankfurter Alle and south along Sonnenalle, toward the Belle-Alliance-Platz and near the Potsdamer Platz, which was in view of the Reichstag. Fighting in this area raged as ideologically motivated Waffen-SS soldiers fought from building to building and room to room. At huge cost Soviet soldiers, supported by their armored units, inched their way forward into the furnace of gunfire and shelling. Over the next 24 hours, bitter fighting raged involving several brutal hand-to-hand actions. Losses on both sides were significant, but the fighting continued with unabated ferocity.

During the early morning of April 29, the 3rd Shock Army reported it had crossed the Moltke Bridge and was assaulting government buildings, including the Ministry of the Interior. However, resistance here was fierce and the lack of Soviet artillery support meant that Red Army units had to wait for resupply before resuming their attacks. Later that day they continued several heavy assaults and captured the Gestapo headquarters on Prinz-Albrechtstrasse, but then came to a halt against heavy resistance. Simultaneously, in the southwest, the 8th Guards Army attacked north toward the Landwehr Canal and then deployed in the direction of Tiergarten Park.

Soviet armor, artillery, trucks, and troops regroup in the devasted central district of Berlin.

In Profile:
Red Army Riflemen and Katyusha Rocket Battery

Riflemen, 79th Rifle Corps, Fürstenwalde, April 20, 1945 (Renato Dalmaso)

A squad of Soviet riflemen prior to being given their orders for the day. They wear a variety of kit including woolen greatcoats, *telogreika* (padded jackets) and standard *gimnasterka* jackets and *portupeya* belts. They wear *pilotka* (field caps with red star) and *ushanka* (fur hats). They are armed with a variety of weapons, including the PPSh-41, the Mosin–Nagant M1938 carbine, and the PPD-34 submachine gun.

Katyusha Rocket Battery, 75th Rocket Launcher Regiment, 47th Army, Bohnsdorf, Berlin, April 21, 1945. (Renato Dalmaso)

Soviet artillerymen arming the Katyusha rocket launcher with 132 mm M-132 rockets for a fire mission in a street. The launcher is a BM-13N Katyusha modified on a Lend-Lease Studebaker US6 2½-ton 6 × 6 truck.

In Profile:
Marshal Konstantin Rokossovsky
December 21, 1896–August 3, 1968

Rokossovsky was regarded as an efficient, hard-working, and gifted commander and was one of the main architects of the Red Army's victory over the Third Reich. He planned and took part in the encirclement of Stalingrad in 1942. The following year his forces repelled the German Army Group Center offensive at Kursk where he skillfully deprived the enemy of any chance of penetrating his defenses. In the summer of 1944, he contributed to the "Soviet blitzkrieg" where he led the 1st Belorussian Front during Operation *Bagration*. Following the destruction of the German central front he was awarded the title of Marshal of the Soviet Union. Through the summer and winter of 1944, he successfully directed his army through Poland toward Germany. However, in November he was suddenly given the command of the 2nd Belorussian Front. Perturbed, he telephoned Stalin and asked why he had been moved from the main area of operations to a secondary sector. Stalin quickly rebuked the marshal and told him curtly that he had been given the new command because he would be directing his army for the decisive operation against Berlin along with the 1st Belorussian and 1st Ukrainian Fronts. In the eyes of Rokossovsky,

he thought he had been given the order to prepare operations to advance and take Berlin. However, that chance quickly vanished when he received a phone call from Stalin telling him that Zhukov would take Berlin. Instead, his forces were to destroy resistance in East Prussia and Pomerania and prevent the German 3rd Panzer Army from taking part in the defense of Berlin.

A column of T-34 tanks advances on a relatively intact Berlin street. In the northwestern outskirts of the city, German forces put up stubborn resistance and managed to temporarily halt the Soviet advance into the central district.

A column of T-34 tanks of the 1st Guards Tank Brigade in the city suburbs.

Among the ruins of Berlin, a Katyusha rocket crew prepare to move to another position.

A battery of Katyusha rocket launchers in action in Berlin.

Soviet SU-176 self-propelled guns on the move in Berlin.

The defense of the German capital was now quickly spiraling out of control. The relief operation in which Hitler had pinned his hope was lost. The German 12th Army could no longer continue its attack toward Berlin, the 9th Army was completely encircled, despite a panzer group breaking out west, and Steiner's corps had been blunted. To make matters worse, General Heinrici had been relieved of his command after disobeying Hitler's direct orders to hold Berlin at all costs. But despite him being replaced temporarily by General Kurt von Tippelskirch, nothing could avert the military situation. Army Group Vistula was almost non-existent as a fighting force and Heinrici's replacement could do nothing but watch the Red Army conquer Berlin.

Inside the doomed city, the Soviets launched their attack against the Reichstag at dawn on April 30. However, due to stiff German resistance, it was not until the evening that Soviet infantry began storming the building. What followed was intense room-to-room fighting.

Elsewhere, in the central district of Berlin, fighting continued with unabated ferocity as some 10,000 German soldiers were assaulted from all sides. One of the main attacks was undertaken along the Wilhelmstrasse where the Air Ministry was situated. Both the 3rd Shock Army and 8th Guards Army closed in around Tiergarten and effectively prevented thousands of German troops from escaping.

An IS-2 Soviet tank stopped in the ravaged central district of Berlin.

German Order of Battle, Berlin, April 21–May 2, 1945

LVI Panzer Corps

Panzer Division Müncheberg

9th Fallschirmjäger Division

18th Panzergrenadier Division

20th Panzergrenadier Division

Kampfgruppe Mohnke (2,000 soldiers)

Begleit Bataillon Reichsführer-SS (600 soldiers)

Führer-Begleit-Kompanie

LSSAH Ausbildungs-und Ersatz Battalion

15th Waffen-Grenadier-Division der SS (company)

11th SS-Freiwilligen-Panzergrenadier-Division Nordland

SS-Einsatz Zquerra (Spanish) (100–150 soldiers)

33rd Waffen-Grenadier-Division der SS Charlemagne (120–300 soldiers)

1st SS-Panzer-Division Leibstandarte Adolf Hitler LAH (600 soldiers)

Wachbattailon Grossdeutschland

Transport-Begleit-Bataillon der Luftwaffe 1/III

Wachbattailon Hermann Göring

Polizei-Regiment Biesenthal

HJ-Abteilung Herbert Norkus

SA-Brigade 28 Horst Wessel (Berlin-Ost)

SA-Bataillon Horst Wessel

SA-Abteilung Wilhelm Gustloff

SA-Brigade 29 (Berlin-Nord)

SA-Brigade 30 (Berlin-West)

SA-Brigade 31 (Berlin-Süd)

SA-Brigade 32 (Berlin-Mitte)

Panzerjagdverband Adolf Hitler

Bataillon 3/115 (Siemensstadt)

503rd SS Heavy Panzer Battalion

1st Flak Division

Volkssturm

SS-Standarte 6

In Profile:
Soviet IS-2 Tank and ISU-152 Assault Gun

IS-2 Tank, 7th Guards Independent Heavy Tank Brigade, Berlin, April 27, 1945. (Oliver Missing)

This heavy tank is painted in overall olive-green with the typical white-stripe markings that were synonymous with the Berlin operation. The vehicle also has the distinctive red star and polar bear logo for the unit's tactical symbol painted on the side of the turret. The polar bear symbol was in acknowledgment of their earlier victory in the Karelian campaign, fighting in the southeastern suburbs of Berlin with the 8th Guards Army.

ISU-152 Assault Gun, 12th Guards Tank Corps, 2nd Guards Tank Army, Tiergarten Park, Berlin, April 29, 1945. (Oliver Missing)

This heavy assault gun is painted in overall olive-green with the Berlin operation white-stripe markings across its fixed turret. Its tactical number "1161" is painted in bold white.

An IS-2 tank appears to have been knocked out. During the night of April 26/27, 2nd Guards Tank units carried out strikes over the Spree, west of the Jungfernheide Station.

A stationary SU-76 on a Berlin street. On April 27 the 8th Guards and 1st Guards Tank Armies attacked northwest along the southern bank of the Landwehr Canal toward Berlin's central Tiergarten Park.

A column of SU-85Ms self-propelled guns on a congested Berlin street poised to move into the central district, April 28.

101

Soviet artillery bombards the central district of Berlin. Throughout April 28 the 8th Guards Army, supported by the 1st Guards Tank Army's 8th Guards Mechanized Corps, fought continuously northwest of the city to linkup with the 3rd Shock Army around the Reichstag.

An ISU-152 tank destroyer paused in a rubble-strewn Berlin street. With its massive 152 mm gun, it proved devastating to German armor.

A battery of Soviet artillery, April 29. On this day the 3rd Shock Army's battle for the Reichstag commenced. The Reichstag building was one of the most important landmarks in the central sector.

Wounded Soviet soldiers being carried away. During the Berlin strategic offensive operation, the Red Army had what were known as mobile front hospital groups, which moved up directly behind the attacking troops and transferred the wounded to special field medical points.

A column of Soviet T-34-tanks in the central district of Berlin, 30 April.

Victorious Red Army troops on a T-34-85 at the Brandenburg Gate. Despite the area being captured, fighting continued to rage throughout the night of May 1/2. Units of the 3rd Shock Army's 79th Rifle Corps linked up in the area south of the Reichstag with units of the 8th Guards Army's 4th Guards Rifle Corps. The 2nd Guards Tank Army's 12th Guards Tank Corps linked up with units of the 8th Guards Army's 28th Guards Rifle Corps and the 1st Guards Tank Army's 8th Guards Mechanized Corps in the western part of the Tiergarten Park. The 2nd Guards Tank Army's 1st Mechanized Corps then linked up with units of the 3rd Guards Tank and 28th Armies around Savigny Station.

Soviet T-34-85 tanks in the central district of Berlin, May 1 or 2. It is unclear what the two wagons are, possibly rail wagons of some sort.

A destroyed German Hummel in the city.

Utter devastation inside the central district of Berlin: destroyed German vehicles and dead soldiers are scattered about.

A sorry group of German POWs with civilian women in tow. Two of the POWs are wounded.

Just after midnight on May 2 the radio station of the 8th Guards Army's 79th Guards Rifle Division picked up a radiogram in Russian from the LVI Panzer Corps: "Hello, hello, this is the LVI Panzer Corps speaking. We request that you cease fire. By 12:50 Berlin time, we are sending envoys to the Potsdam Bridge. The recognition sign will be a white flag on a red background. We await your reply." Here Red Army IS-2 tanks are halted following the German surrender. The Reichstag is in the background; the flag on top would be the hammer and sickle.

Soviet Order of Battle, Berlin, April 21– May 2, 1945

1ST BELORUSSIAN FRONT (Zhukov)

47th Army (no details of commander)

125th Rifle Corps
(No details of subunits)

175th Rifle Corps
76th Rifle Division
185th Rifle Division
60th Rifle Division

129th Rifle Corps
146th Rifle Division
82nd Rifle Division
132nd Rifle Division

Artillery etc.
334th Guards Heavy Self-Propelled Artillery Regiment
1204th Self-Propelled Artillery Regiment
1416th Self-Propelled Artillery Regiment
1892nd Self-Propelled Artillery Regiment
6th Breakthrough Artillery Division
2nd Mortar Brigade
10th Cannon Artillery Brigade
18th Howitzer Artillery Brigade
21st Light Artillery Brigade
118th Heavy Howitzer Artillery Brigade
124th Howitzer Artillery Brigade
4th Corps Artillery Brigade
74th Anti-Aircraft Artillery Division
18th Engineer Brigade
70th Independent Guard Heavy Tank Regiment

3rd Shock Army (Kuznetsov)

79th Rifle Corps
150th Rifle Division
171st Rifle Division
207th Rifle Division

12th Guards Rifle Corps
23rd Guards Rifle Division
33rd Rifle Division
52nd Guards Rifle Division

7th Rifle Corps
146th Rifle Division
265th Rifle Division
364th Rifle Division

38th Rifle Corps
52nd Rifle Division
64th Rifle Division
89th Rifle Division

9th Tank Corps
23rd Tank Brigade

95th Tank Brigade

108th Tank Brigade

8th Motorized Rifle Brigade

85th Independent Tank Regiment

88th Independent Guards Heavy Tank Regiment

Artillery etc.

351st Guards Heavy Self-Propelled Artillery Regiment

1049th Self-Propelled Artillery Regiment

1203rd Self-Propelled Artillery Regiment

1445th Self-Propelled Artillery Regiment

1508th Self-Propelled Artillery Regiment

1728th Self-Propelled Artillery Regiment

1729th Self-Propelled Artillery Regiment

1818th Self-Propelled Artillery Regiment

4th Breakthrough Artillery Corps

5th Breakthrough Artillery Division

1st Mortar Brigade

9th Howitzer Artillery Brigade

24th Cannon Artillery Brigade

86th Heavy Howitzer Artillery Brigade

100th Howitzer Artillery Brigade

12th Breakthrough Artillery Division

41st Guards Mortar Brigade

89th Heavy Howitzer Artillery Brigade

104th Howitzer Artillery Brigade

40th Independent Tank-Destroyer Artillery Brigade

45th Tank-Destroyer Artillery Brigade

136th Army Cannon Artillery Brigade

5th Guards Mortar Division

16th Guards Mortar Brigade

22nd Guards Mortar Brigade

23rd Guards Mortar Brigade

19th Anti-Aircraft Artillery Division

25th Engineer Brigade

5th Shock Army (Berzarin)

26th Guards Rifle Corps

89th Guards Rifle Division

94th Guards Rifle Division

266th Rifle Division

32nd Rifle Corps

60th Guards Rifle Division

295th Rifle Division

416th Rifle Division

9th Rifle Corps

230th Rifle Division

248th Rifle Division

301st Rifle Division

11th Tank Corps

20th Tank Brigade

36th Tank Brigade

65th Tank Brigade

12th Motorized Rifle Brigade

11th Independent Guards Heavy Tank Brigade

67th Guards Heavy Tank Brigade

220th Independent Tank Brigade

Artillery etc.

396th Guards Heavy Self-Propelled Artillery Regiment

1504th Independent Self-Propelled Artillery Regiment

6th Breakthrough Artillery Corps

2nd Breakthrough Artillery Division

5th Mortar Brigade

10th Guards Howitzer Artillery Brigade

16th Guards Cannon Artillery Brigade

20th Light Artillery Brigade

48th Guards Heavy Howitzer Artillery Brigade

121st Howitzer Artillery Brigade

14th Breakthrough Artillery Division

6th Guards Mortar Brigade

21st Heavy Mortar Brigade

24th Mortar Brigade

122nd Howitzer Artillery Brigade

169th Light Artillery Brigade

172nd Howitzer Artillery Brigade

22nd Breakthrough Artillery Division

6th Heavy Mortar Brigade

32nd Mortar Brigade

97th Heavy Howitzer Brigade

2nd Guards Mortar Brigade

25th Guards Mortar Brigade

35th Guards Mortar Brigade

2nd Guards Anti-Aircraft Artillery Division

1st Independent Guards Motorized Engineer Brigade

17th Breakthrough Engineer Brigade

61st Engineer Brigade

8th Guards Army (Chuikov)

4th Guards Rifle Corps

35th Guards Rifle Division

47th Guards Rifle Division

57th Guards Rifle Division

29th Guards Rifle Corps

27th Guards Rifle Division

74th Guards Rifle Division

82nd Guards Rifle Division

28th Guards Rifle Corps

39th Guards Rifle Division

79th Guards Rifle Division

88th Guards Rifle Division

7th Independent Guards Heavy Tank Brigade

34th Independent Guards Heavy Tank Regiment

65th Independent Tank Regiment

259th Independent Tank Regiment

Artillery etc.

371st Guards Self-Propelled Artillery Regiment

394th Guards Heavy Self-Propelled Artillery Regiment

394th Guards Heavy Self-Propelled Artillery Regiment

694th Self-Propelled Artillery Regiment

1026th Self-Propelled Artillery Regiment

1061st Self-Propelled Artillery Regiment

1087th Self-Propelled Artillery Regiment

1200th Self-Propelled Artillery Regiment

3rd Breakthrough Artillery Corps

18th Breakthrough Artillery Division

2nd Heavy Howitzer Artillery Brigade

42nd Mortar Brigade

58th Howitzer Artillery Brigade

65th Light Artillery Brigade

80th Heavy Howitzer Artillery Brigade

120th Howitzer Artillery Brigade

29th Breakthrough Artillery Division

26th Heavy Mortar Brigade

36th Guards Mortar Brigade

46th Mortar Brigade

182nd Light Artillery Brigade

184th Howitzer Artillery Brigade

186th Howitzer Artillery Brigade

189th Heavy Howitzer Artillery Brigade

38th Tank-Destroyer Artillery Brigade

43rd Army Guards Cannon Artillery Brigade

2nd Guards Mortar Division

17th Guards Mortar Brigade

20th Guards Mortar Brigade

26th Guards Mortar Brigade

3rd Guards Anti-Aircraft Artillery Division

2nd Breakthrough Engineer Brigade

7th Pontoon Bridge Brigade

64th Engineer Brigade

1st Guards Tank Army (Dremov)

11th Guards Tank Corps

40th Guards Tank Brigade

44th Guards Tank Brigade

45th Guards Tank Brigade

27th Guards Motorized Rifle Brigade

8th Guards Mechanized Corps

19th Guards Mechanized Brigade

20th Guards Mechanized Brigade

21st Guards Mechanized Brigade

1st Guards Tank Brigade

64th Independent Guards Tank Brigade

11th Independent Guards Heavy Tank Regiment

48th Independent Guards Heavy Tank Regiment

Artillery etc.

19th Self-Propelled Artillery Brigade

353rd Guards Self-Propelled Artillery Regiment

362nd Guards Heavy Self-Propelled Artillery Regiment

399th Guards Heavy Self-Propelled Artillery Regiment

400th Guards Self-Propelled Artillery Regiment

145th Self-Propelled Artillery Regiment

25th Independent Tank-Destroyer Artillery Brigade

41st Tank-Destroyer Artillery Brigade

197th Light Artillery Brigade

4th Guards Anti-Aircraft Artillery Division

6th Pontoon Bridge Brigade

17th Motorized Engineer Brigade

2nd Guards Tank Army (Sinenko)

12th Guards Tank Corps

48th Guards Tank Brigade

49th Guards Tank Brigade

34th Guards Motorized Rifle Division

1st Polish Infantry Division

1st Mechanized Brigade

35th Mechanized Brigade

37th Mechanized Brigade

219th Tank Brigade

33rd Guards Motorized Rifle Brigade

9th Guards Tank Corps

6th Independent Guards Heavy Tank Regiment

79th Independent Guards Heavy Tank Regiment

75th Self-Propelled Artillery Regiment

347th Guards Heavy Self-Propelled Artillery Regiment

393rd Guards Self-Propelled Artillery Regiment

2nd Polish Howitzer Artillery Brigade

20th Tank-Destroyer Artillery Brigade

198th Light Artillery Brigade

24th Anti-Aircraft Artillery Division

18th Motorized Engineer Brigade

16th Air Army (Rudenko)

1st Guards Fighter Aviation Corps

3rd Guards Fighter Aviation Division

4th Guards Fighter Aviation Division

3rd Fighter Aviation Corps

265th Fighter Aviation Division

278th Fighter Aviation Division

3rd Bomber Aviation Corps

241st Bomber Aviation Division

301st Bomber Aviation Division

183rd Bomber Aviation Division

6th Bomber Aviation Corps

113th Bomber Aviation Division

326th Bomber Aviation Division

6th Assault Aviation Corps

197th Assault Aviation Division

198th Assault Aviation Division

6th Fighter Aviation Corps

234th Fighter Aviation Division

273rd Fighter Aviation Division

9th Assault Aviation Corps

3rd Guards Assault Aviation Division

300th Assault Aviation Division

13th Fighter Aviation Corps

193rd Fighter Aviation Division

283rd Fighter Aviation Division

1st Guards Fighter Aviation Division

(no details of Corps)

9th Guards Night Bomber Aviation Division

11th Guards Assault Aviation Division

188th Bomber Aviation Division

221st Bomber Aviation Division

242nd Night Bomber Aviation Division

282nd Fighter Aviation Division

286th Fighter Aviation Division

1ST UKRAINIAN FRONT (Konev)

28th Army (Luchinsky)

20th Rifle Corps

20th Rifle Division

48th Guards Rifle Division

55th Guards Rifle Division

128th Rifle Corps

61st Rifle Division

152nd Rifle Division

Artillery etc.

25th Breakthrough Artillery Division

3rd Guards Mortar Brigade

39th Mortar Brigade

48th Heavy Mortar Brigade

175th Light Artillery Brigade

181st Heavy Howitzer Artillery Brigade

183rd Howitzer Artillery Brigade

31st Breakthrough Artillery Division

35th Mortar Brigade

51st Heavy Mortar Brigade

191st Howitzer Artillery Brigade

194th Heavy Howitzer Artillery Brigade

8th Independent Guards Tank-Destroyer Artillery Brigade

157th Army Cannon Artillery Brigade

71st Anti-Aircraft Artillery Division

36th Engineer Brigade

3rd Guards Tank Army (Rybalko)

9th Mechanized Brigade

69th Mechanized Brigade

70th Mechanized Brigade

71st Mechanized Brigade

91st Tank Brigade

6th Guards Tank Corps

51st Guards Tank Brigade

52nd Guards Tank Brigade

53rd Guards Tank Brigade

22nd Guards Motorized Rifle Brigade

7th Guards Tank Corps

54th Guards Tank Brigade

55th Guards Tank Brigade

56th Guards Tank Brigade

23rd Guards Motorized Rifle Brigade

57th Independent Guards Heavy Tank Regiment

384th Guards Heavy Tank Regiment

Artillery etc.

16th Self-Propelled Artillery Brigade

702nd Self-Propelled Artillery Regiment

1507th Self-Propelled Artillery Regiment

1893rd Self-Propelled Artillery Regiment

1977th Self-Propelled Artillery Regiment

1978th Self-Propelled Artillery Regiment

4th Breakthrough Artillery Division

30th Guards Mortar Brigade

37th Mortar Brigade

49th Heavy Mortar Brigade

50th Guards Heavy Howitzer Brigade

163rd Howitzer Artillery Brigade

168th Light Artillery Brigade

171st Howitzer Artillery Brigade

23rd Anti-Aircraft Artillery Division

19th Motorized Engineer Brigade

4th Guards Tank Army (Lelyushenko)

10th Guards Tank Corps

62nd Guards Tank Brigade

63rd Guards Tank Brigade

70th Guards Self-Propelled Artillery Brigade

71st Independent Guards Light Artillery Brigade

6th Guards Anti-Aircraft Artillery Division

2nd Air Army (Krasovsky)

2nd Guards Assault Aviation Corps
5th Guards Assault Aviation Division
11th Guards Fighter Aviation Division

6th Guards Bomber Aviation Corps
1st Guards Bomber Aviation Division
8th Guards Bomber Aviation Division

2nd Fighter Aviation Corps
7th Guards Fighter Aviation Division
322nd Fighter Aviation Division

6th Guards Fighter Aviation Corps
9th Guards Fighter Aviation Division
23rd Guards Fighter Aviation Division

4th Bomber Aviation Corps
219th Bomber Aviation Division
256th Fighter Aviation Division

5th Fighter Aviation Corps
(No details of subunits)

18th Air Army (no details of commander)

1st Guards Bomber Aviation Corps
11th Guards Bomber Aviation Division
16th Guards Bomber Aviation Division
36th Bomber Aviation Division
48th Bomber Aviation Division

2nd Guards Bomber Aviation Corps
2nd Guards Bomber Aviation Division
7th Guards Bomber Aviation Division
13th Guards Bomber Aviation Division

3rd Guards Bomber Aviation Corps
1st Guards Bomber Aviation Division
12th Bomber Aviation Division
22nd Guards Bomber Aviation Division
50th Bomber Aviation Division
14th Bomber Aviation Division

4th Guards Bomber Aviation Corps
45th Bomber Aviation Division

In Profile:
Soviet Katyusha Rocket Launcher and T-34-85 Tank

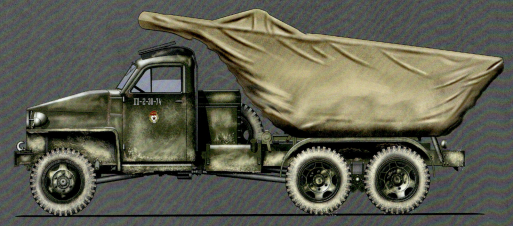

Katuysha Rocket Launcher, 75th Rocket Launcher Regiment, 47th Army, Berlin, April 30, 1945. (Oliver Missing)

This BM-13N Katyusha rocket launcher modified on a Lend-Lease Studebaker US6 2½-ton 6 × 6 truck is painted in overall olive-green. The vehicle is in transport and tarpaulin protects the rocket launcher.

T-34-85 Tank, 1st Mechanized Corps, 2nd Guards Tank Army, Savigny Station, Berlin, May 1, 1945. (Oliver Missing)

This tank is painted in overall olive-green and has the distinctive Berlin operation white-stripe markings painted horizontally across its turret and laterally on part of the cupola. The tactical number "183" is painted in bold white.

| Aftermath

During the early hours of May 1 with fighting in the city center still raging, General Hans Krebs, chief of the German High Command of the Wehrmacht, left the Führerbunker, entombed 50 feet below the Reich Chancellery, and delivered a written letter under a white flag to Marshal Vasily Chuikov, commander of the Soviet 8th Guards Army. The letter outlined surrender terms, but these terms were immediately rejected. The Red Army, he told Krebs, would only accept unconditional surrender. Krebs went on to tell the Soviet general of Hitler's suicide in the bunker, and then left and returned to the bunker. With the suicide of Joseph Goebbels that morning, the responsibility of surrender fell to the commander of Berlin Defense Area, General Helmuth Weidling.

On May 2, as the Germans were losing complete control of the city center, Red Army intelligence began receiving urgent radio messages from the German LVI Armored Corps requesting surrender. To discuss the surrender of the city, General Weidling was taken to Schulenburgring 2 in Berlin-Tempelhof where Chuikov had set up his field headquarters. Following a short discussion, Weidling signed the order of surrender of the Berlin garrison, finally ending the enormous loss of life inside the devastated city.

Elsewhere, battles around Berlin continued, even though the capital garrison had surrendered. Remnants of Army Group Vistula were still fighting in several areas. In the Halbe region troops of the 9th Army who had crawled out of the inferno alive moved west.

Following the end of the battle inside Berlin, a Soviet rifle unit marches along a street with commander holding the Soviet flag in recognition of victory over the Nazis.

Berliners among the ruins, with the corpse of a German soldier in the foreground.

Emerging from a subway, German troops surrender their weapons.

Soviet soldiers rejoice following the end of hostilities inside the capital.

A long column of German POWs marching east into captivity. In the background is the Bahnhof Yorck Straße Bridge.

Two photographs taken in sequence showing German POWs trudging past a stationary T-34-85 tank in Berlin. Several are wounded, their chances of survival negligible.

German POWs march past Berlin civilians gathered along the street.

A fine photograph of Red Army troops and their young boy-soldier mascot in front of the Reichstag following its capture.

An elderly cyclist negotiates destroyed vehicles littering a street, followed by a nonchalant schoolboy.

117

Desperate Volkssturm POWs prepare to carry their wounded comrade, whose chances of survival are zero. In the middle is a soldier whose whole face is bandaged. The women in the background are equally desperate, their faces gaunt.

The 21st Army, after breaking out of its Elbe bridgehead, managed to reach the Baltic coast at Lübeck and Wismar only to surrender its disintegrated forces to the Americans. The 3rd Panzer Army was forced to retreat into the region of Mecklenburg and on May 3 surrendered to the British, rather than capitulating 300,000 of its remaining exhausted and disheveled troops to the Soviets.

A Soviet IS-2 crew pose on their tank.

A Soviet soldier smokes a cigarette among the ruins of Berlin.

Soviet soldiers next to a knocked-out German flak gun which had been positioned in front of the Reichstag for defense purposes.

Berlin civilians struggle through a rubble-strewn street.

Soviet soldiers dish out soup to Berlin civilians. Across the city over a million people were homeless and many were starving. Starvation continued to be a major problem months after the capture of the city.

The same day, the 12th Army, which had been fighting in the Potsdam area with remnants of the 9th Army, negotiated surrender terms with the Americans. Between May 5–7 both the 12th and 9th Armies withdrew across the Elbe and took refuge behind the American lines where they finally surrendered.

With German forces crushed or capitulated, the Berlin strategic offensive operation was complete. The operation was more than just the battle of Berlin, and the loss of life preparing the final attack into the city was far greater than fighting inside the capital itself. The Soviet victory was a victory of complete ruthlessness but was equally astonishing in both strategic and tactical planning. The offensive against Berlin was an operation of extreme nature. It guaranteed the Soviet leadership a string of unbroken victories, from the Seelow Heights to the complete encirclement of the city and the final battles that ensued inside the city.

The five phases that were part of the strategic operation were more important than the defeat of Berlin itself. The already-doomed capital had few

Soviet officers inspect dead Volkssturm.

Above: A Soviet officer reads out orders to his troops.

Left: Captured teenage Hitlerjugend soldiers stand looking perplexed. They have been ordered to remove their battle kit.

In a staged photograph, Soviet soldiers in Hitler's Reich Chancellery garden point to where Hitler's burned remains were found following his suicide.

121

Following the capture of the central district of Berlin, civilians emerge from a subway. Scattered on the sidewalk next to the German POWs is discarded battle gear.

defensive structures and measures implemented for the Stavka to be concerned about. The most important factors of the battle were Zhukov's 1st Belorussian Front reaching the fortified Seelow Heights, Rokossovsky's 2nd Belorussian Front supporting Zhukov from the south, and Konev's 1st Ukrainian Front advancing in the Cottbus area and south of Berlin to destroy the German defense. But the main focal point of the offensive had been given to the 1st Belorussian Front. However, the operation would have not been possible without the support of the 2nd Belorussian and 1st Ukrainian Fronts. There were also many defensive areas in front of Berlin that were vitally important to be captured first to secure each phase successfully, and this could not have been achieved so quickly without the three army fronts. Vital road and rail links needed to be secured, and German formations needed to be prevented from regrouping and defending various towns that were being turned into "fortresses." The Soviets knew that the German leadership recognized the threat to Berlin and was responding decisively in building up their defenses. The Soviet operation was an offensive of a series of advances and encirclements.

As a result of the operation, the Germans were defeated, which saw the suicide of Hitler and the downfall of Nazism. It was an outstanding victory for the Red Army. The battle had been a true test of the strength of two different ideologies which had, by 1945, seen the German war machine sapped of most its strength. It was no longer able to sustain itself cohesively on the battlefield against an overwhelming army. In the end, the Red Army brought to Germany the pain and misery that the Germans themselves had inflicted on Russia, and won decisively.

A Soviet soldier on a bicycle overtakes Berlin civilians, now refugees with their meager possessions. Civilian bicycles were much prized by the Red Army troops.

German troops who have just surrendered are led away under armed guard past a stationary T-34-85 tank. It appears the battle has only just finished.

German POWs check out a T-34-85 tank passing them.

Soviet soldiers pose following the capture of Berlin. The soldier standing and the man on the right are armed with the German MP 40 submachine gun, which was very popular with Red Army troops.

The crew of an SU-76 take the salute during a parade through a Berlin street following the capture of the city. In total some 6,300 tanks and self-propelled artillery pieces took part in the battle for Berlin.

An aerial view of the destruction wrought on the central district of Berlin, with the Brandenburg Gate in the foreground.

| Further Reading

Baxter, Ian. *The East Pomeranian Offensive, 1945: Destruction of German forces in Pomerania and West Prussia*. Oxford, United Kingdom & Philadelphia, PA: Casemate Publishers, 2025.

Baxter, Ian. *The Soviet Baltic Offensive, 1944–45: German Defense of Estonia, Latvia, and Lithuania*. Oxford, United Kingdom & Philadelphia, PA: Casemate Publishers, 2022.

Baxter, Ian. *The Soviet Destruction of Army Group South: Ukraine and Southern Poland 1943–1945*. Oxford, United Kingdom & Philadelphia, PA: Casemate Publishers, 2023.

Baxter, Ian. *The Vistula-Oder Offensive: The Soviet Destruction of German Army Group A, 1945*. Oxford, United Kingdom & Philadelphia, PA: Casemate Publishers, 2024.

Beevor, Antony. *Berlin: The Downfall 1945*. London: Viking, 2002.

Cornish, Nik. *Berlin: Victory in Europe*. Barnsley, United Kingdom: Pen & Sword Books, 2010.

Glantz, David M. *Forgotten Battles of the German–Soviet War (1941–1945), Vol. V: The Summer–Fall Campaign (1 July–December 1943)* Part II. Self-Published, 2000.

Glantz, David M. *Soviet Military Intelligence in War*. London & Portland, OR: Frank Cass, 1990.

Grechko, A. A., Marshal (ed.). *Istoriya Vtoroy Mirovoy Voyny 1939–1945* (History of the Second World War 1939–1945) Vol. 3. Moscow: Voyenizdat, 1974.

Harrison, Richard W. *The Development of Russian-Soviet Operational Art, 1904–1937 and the Imperial Legacy in Soviet Military Thought*. London: Department of War Studies, King's College, University of London, 1994.

Heiber, Helmut & Glantz, David M. (eds.). *Hitler and His Generals: Military Conferences, 1942–1945*. London: Greenhill Books, 2002 (Original German publication 1966).

Le Tissier, Tony. *The Battle of Berlin, 1945*. Cheltenham, United Kingdom: The History Press, 2022.

Le Tissier, Tony. *Death Was Our Companion: The Final Days of the Third Reich*. Cheltenham, United Kingdom: The History Press, 2021.

Le Tissier, Tony. *Marshal Zhukov at the Oder: The Decisive Battle for Berlin*, Cheltenham, United Kingdom: The History Press, 2021.

Le Tissier, Tony. *Slaughter at Halbe: The Destruction of Hitler's 9th Army*. Cheltenham, United Kingdom: The History Press, 2021.

Le Tissier, Tony. *With Our Backs to Berlin: The German Army in Retreat 1945*. Cheltenham, United Kingdom: The History Press, 2021.

Nebolsin, Igor & Britton, Stuart (ed.). *Stalin's Favorite: The Combat History of the 2nd Guards Tank Army from Kursk to Berlin: Vol 2: From Lublin to Berlin July 1944–May 1945*. Warwick, United Kingdom: Helion & Co., 2016.

Soviet General Staff. *The Berlin Operation*. Edited and translated by Richard W. Harrison. Warwick, United Kingdom: Helion & Co., 2016. Published in cooperation with the Association of the United States Army.

Tieke, Wilhelm. *Between the Oder and the Elbe: The Opening Moves in the Battle for Berlin, 1945*. Barnsley, United Kingdom: Pen & Sword Books, 2024.

Tucker-Jones, Anthony. *The Fall of Berlin: The Final Days of Hitler's Evil Regime*. London: Arcturus Publishing, 2024.

Vasilevskiy, A. "Belorusskaya Stratgiskaya Operatskaya" (The Belorussian Strategic Operation) in *Voyenno Istoricheskiy Zhurnal* No. 10, October 1969.

| Index